THE RISE OF HIS HOLY ONES

UNVEILING THE POWER OF THE SPIRIT OF HOLINESS

MICHAEL FICKESS

COMPLETE WITH SMALL GROUP DISCUSSION QUESTIONS

Jessie,
You are deeply loved by the Lord and a precious jewel in His heart.
Shalom,
Michael

Other books by Michael Fickess:

Enoch's Blessing

Paths of Ever-Increasing Glory

Start the Countdown

The Restoration of All Things

CSCL Bible Curriculum Series

Endorsements for *The Rise of His Holy Ones*

This book will be treasured manna for all who are in pursuit of God—those who want to know Him and see His glory restored to the earth. One of the greatest gifts we can have is a hunger for God that keeps us seeking Him. This work will impart a greater desire for Him and light the path that leads to a closer relationship with Him.

– Rick Joyner
Founder and President, MorningStar Ministries

The Rise of His Holy Ones will challenge you to reexamine your walk with God while further grasping the holiness of the Most High. In this book, Michael Fickess provides an end-time prophetic perspective of God's glory, resurrection power, and the five-fold ministry operating through holiness. To better understand the power of the spirit of holiness and its effect in the earth today, I encourage you to read *The Rise of His Holy Ones*. You won't be disappointed.

– Bonnie Jones
Bob and Bonnie Jones Ministries

Over a summer I delved into Augustine's classic, *The City of God*, a 1600-year-old apologetic work contrasting the kingdom of God with the kingdom of darkness and the kingdoms of this world. As I read this book, I noticed some striking parallels. *The Rise of His Holy Ones* contains biblical teaching and visionary experiences that reveal God's plan to endue His people with light and glory in the time of increasing darkness. In this book, you will hear the call to join the ranks of this company of Holy Ones, who are increasing in hunger and anointing. Not only did I thoroughly enjoy reading this book, it continually provoked me to go higher in pursuit of friendship and encounter with God.

– Justin Perry
Lead Pastor, MorningStar Fellowship Church

The Rise of His Holy Ones
by Michael Fickess
Copyright ©2017

First Edition

Distributed by MorningStar Publications, Inc.,
a division of MorningStar Fellowship Church
375 Star Light Drive, Fort Mill, SC 29715
www.MorningStarMinistries.org
1-800-542-0278

Unless otherwise indicated, all Scripture quotations are taken from Holy Bible, New King James Version (NKJV), copyright 1982 by HarperCollins Publishers.

All quotations from the Book of Enoch are taken from *Enoch's Blessing: A Modern English Paraphrase of Enoch's Ancient Writings*, copyright 2014 by Michael Fickess.

No part of this book may be reproduced or transmitted in any form or by any means electronic or mechanical, including photocopying, recording, or by any information storage and retrieval system, without written permission from the author.

All rights reserved.

Printed in the United States of America.
Cover Design by Michael Fickess
Layout Design by Michael R. Carter

ISBN— 978-1-60708-690-1; 1-60708-690-5

For a free catalog of MorningStar Resources, please call 1-800-542-0278

Table of Contents

INTRODUCTION
-7-

EXPLORING THE MYSTERIES OF HOLINESS
-9-

ONE: *When Lightning Strikes*
-11-

TWO: *The Spirit of Holiness*
-20-

THREE: *Rediscovering Holiness*
-28-

WHEN HIS HOLY ONES ASSEMBLE
-49-

FOUR: *The Coming Mountain of the Lord*
-50-

FIVE: *A Tale of Two Cities*
-62-

SIX: *Ruling and Reigning*
-79-

SEVEN: *The Coming "Christ Ministry"*
-93-

EIGHT: *The Ancient Gatekeepers*
-103-

WALKING WITH THE HOLY ONE
-110-

NINE: *Finding the Highway of Holiness*
-111-

TEN: *The Redemption of Desire*
-122-

ELEVEN: *Cultivating a "Golden Mind"*
-143-

TWELVE: *The Rise of His Living Lightnings*
-163-

THIRTEEN: *The Terror of the Holiness of the Glory*
-175-

Introduction

As I write this today, I hear thunder in the distance. Dark clouds are rolling in and lightning ripples across the horizon. The trees shake as fierce winds descend upon the landscape. The greatest turbulence in all of human history is beginning to unfold. And as this great storm unfolds, a vast body of holy ones will rise to meet the challenge.

These holy ones will carry the light and lightnings of heaven. They will embody the most powerful message of all time—**"Christ and Him crucified"** (see I Corinthians 2:2). As a result, they will rule and reign on the earth, bringing the kingdom of God with power at a time when others tremble with fear and wonder. They will carry a magnitude of wisdom, revelation, and love that previous generations could not imagine. They will provide the antidote to restore the heart of mankind at a time when the kingdoms of this world are crumbling.

My primary purpose in writing this book is to declare the destiny of these "rising holy ones." The ancient prophecies of the Bible reveal that God will raise up an unshakeable kingdom in these times to destroy and displace every other kingdom. However, in order to explore these promises and lay hold of our destiny, we must first dispel every false, shallow notion of holiness keeping us in chains. We must find the deeper streams of holiness that enable us to abide in the presence of the Holy One all the time. When we do this, we become the forerunners for a new expansion of the kingdom of heaven, paving the way for everything that follows.

If these promises stir longing in your heart, it indicates that you are destined to be one of these "rising holy ones." It is time for us to lay hold of everything the Bible says about us, until our lives become a resting place where the Spirit of Holiness is pleased to dwell continually.

A careful study of church history reveals that every move of God comes with a corresponding set of theological blueprints. As God pours out His Spirit with much greater power, we can also expect Him to reveal His Word with much greater clarity. In order to help every reader apply and embody the truths in this book, I have included a set of questions after each chapter. These questions may be used for individual reflection or small group discussion.

This book is similar to my previous book, *Paths of Ever-Increasing Glory*, because it uses prophetic insight to illumine biblical truths for our times. The restorations of truth in every previous move of God will remain critical foundations as we move forward. My goal is to honor those that came before by reiterating their message while clearing the way for much greater restorations of truth in the future.

Exploring the Mysteries of Holiness

When Lightning Strikes   1

The tomb I stood in was a giant chasm in the earth. The air was stale and heavy with the toxic smell of rotting flesh. As my eyes adjusted to the darkness, I saw two things clearly. First, I noticed there were many people around me trapped in the tomb and still alive. Second, I noticed a crack at the top of the tomb that let in just enough light to see what was happening. The people imprisoned there were tethered to the floors and walls of the tomb with iron shackles that chafed their skin and kept them from reaching up.

The light pouring in through the crack in the ceiling was nothing less than otherworldly. It gave hope for restoration when all hope was lost. It gave ailing bodies the power to wake up, stand up, and look up. Although only a sliver of sunlight shone through the crack, those who kept their eyes fixed on it found renewed strength. At first, they could only sit up. Then, they could stand. Last, they could look up and raise their hands to the light. As soon as each one attempted to reach up, their shackles immediately tumbled to the stone floor. It was amazing that those trapped in this tomb had any hope at all, for the sliver of light was several stories above them and there appeared to be no escape from this dark prison.

I was shocked by the resolve of the people who kept their eyes fixed on the light, despite the stench of death and hopelessness that surrounded them. I was even more surprised by what happened next. As the people began to raise their voices and cry out to the Lord, a great bolt of lightning was released from the throne. At the moment the lightning struck, the whole tomb was shaken apart by violent earthquakes and thunders. This bolt of lightning was more than a brief flash—it remained and increased in brilliance and power until its purpose was fully accomplished. The ceiling began to break open, slowly at first with small chunks falling away, revealing a full array of heavenly light rising on the horizon. At this moment, the remaining prisoners were released from their shackles. Soon the rest of the ceiling crumbled and crashed to the ground, revealing a glorious dawn of brilliant color. This dawn was brighter and more beautiful than any of the prisoners could imagine in their former condition.

When the lightning from heaven struck, it accomplished more than destroying the tombs and the chains. The lightning poured in with full and radiant strength, transfiguring the prisoners calling on the Lord to become free and holy people through the resurrection power of Jesus Christ. The lightning surrounded each one, stripping them of filthy rags and clothing them in white linen, which sparkled like freshly fallen snow in the morning sun. Their faces now shone with the same bright white light that liberated them. As I saw them climb out of the tomb, I knew this light would continue to increase on them as they went throughout the earth with the regality of kings marching to war. The former slaves to deception were now dread champions armed with the ultimate truth—the power of Christ's redemption.

The Coming Harvest

When I received this open vision in the summer of 2014, the Spirit of the Lord told me He was taking me to the "tomb of the unknown soldier." As a veteran of the Iraq War, I place the highest honor on my brothers-in-arms, and I mean no disrespect to those who paid the ultimate price. However, the Lord was trying to tell me something: He is about to raise up a holy army of light from a vast throng of people who are currently unknown. Yet, this vast throng of people is currently suffering in the most miserable of spiritual conditions.

As I watched the people in this tomb develop a resolve to find the light, I was keenly aware that this multitude included people who had escaped three specific kinds of bondage. The first group included those in the body of Christ shackled by dead religion and tradition. The second group included the completely unchurched, those living in sin but deeply hungering for a living God they have not yet encountered. The third group included people deceived by counterfeit spirituality, New Age practices, witchcraft, or other occult activities. I was most shocked by how many in this third group streamed to the light of the Lord Jesus Christ and jumped at the opportunity to become holy people who serve Him day and night. This third group was not released from their chains until the lightning fell with full strength.

Until this hour, most of the body of Christ in the United States and Europe has been restrained and bound by religious tradition. For this reason, many of those whom God has called have left the church altogether or have run after false gods. However, the Father is calling a great multitude back into His kingdom. I connect this vision to the prophetic promise of the great harvest of souls. I believe these three groups of people will be among the first saved in the next move of God, and that many of them will lead thousands of people to the Lord as "eleventh-hour workers" when the next move of the Spirit unfolds (see Matthew 20:1-16).

Searching the Scriptures

The Lord embeds biblical symbols and concepts into the revelations He gives because He wants us to be forced to search the Scriptures. Digging deep in the Word allows us to verify the accuracy of what we have seen or heard and discover much more about what the Lord is saying. The same Spirit of Truth who gives us a revelation can also lead us to the most relevant Scriptures for interpreting it and applying it to our lives. As I was in this prophetic experience, my mind kept returning to one of my favorite Bible chapters:

And when Jesus cried out again in a loud voice, he gave up his spirit.
At that moment the curtain of the temple was torn in two from top to bottom. The earth shook and the rocks split.
The tombs broke open and the bodies of many holy people who had died were raised to life.
They came out of their tombs, and after Jesus' resurrection they went into the holy city and appeared to many people.
When the centurion and those with him who were guarding Jesus saw the earthquake and all that had happened, they were terrified and exclaimed, "Surely he was the Son of God!" (Matthew 27:50-54 NIV)

The redemption that Christ completed at the moment He cried out, **"It is finished!"** is more than enough to set multitudes free from dead religion, rebellion, or counterfeit spirituality. However, there is an even greater promise here: Christ's atonement is powerful enough to raise up a vast generation of holy people.

These holy ones will literally walk in all **"the powers of the age to come" (see Hebrews 6:5).** They will see the dawn of the kingdom of God in a manner that no other generation deemed possible. They will have an understanding of the redemption of

Christ that goes much deeper and higher than any previous generation. As a result, they will love God more passionately, more deeply, and more completely than any other generation. We have seen many forerunners walk in the light of the Lord throughout human history—from the ancient patriarchs and prophets to the saints and revivalists of the last few centuries. However, what is different about this final generation is that multitudes from every nation will be made holy (see Revelation 7:9).

Waking Up to be "Children of the Light"

Matthew 27 uses many of the same symbols in my vision: God raised holy people up out of tombs and they went throughout the city to testify of Christ's power and redemption. However, Matthew was describing the raising up of holy people who were physically dead but spiritually alive. I continued to search the Scriptures until I found precisely what I saw unfolding—the raising up of a holy people from among those who are physically alive but spiritually dead. Although this concept may seem strange, Paul describes it clearly:

For you were once darkness, but now you are light in the Lord. Walk as children of light,
for the fruit of the Spirit is in all goodness, righteousness, and truth,
finding out what is acceptable to the Lord.
And have no fellowship with the unfruitful works of darkness, but rather expose them.
For it is shameful even to speak of those things which are done by them in secret.
But all things that are exposed are made manifest by the light, for whatever makes manifest is light.
Therefore He says: "Awake, you who sleep, arise from the dead, and Christ will give you light" (Ephesians 5:8-14).

In this text, Paul tells believers they were once lost in spiritual darkness, but they have now become "children of the light." He describes how the brilliant light of the Lord exposes any areas of bondage in our lives and reveals many things we did not know before. However, the clearest confirmation in this chapter comes from the expression, **"Awake, you who sleep, arise from the dead, and Christ will give you light."**

Those who press in to find a deeper walk with the Lord will become more and more like Him with every passing day.

Paul places this expression in quotes because it was one of the trusted sayings that first-century believers often used to encourage one another. This expression was common in the first century because the early church had a clear understanding of how the light of Christ can resurrect our spirits. They were aware that being "born again" implies a whole new way of living—we leave the spiritual darkness of our past and step into the penetrating and supernatural light of our heavenly Father.

The Bible clearly instructs us to **"walk in the light as He is in the light" (see I John 1:7)**. However, we have not realized how powerful His light is. We first glimpse this light when we are born again, but we do not have to stop there. If we remain in the light all the time as John instructed, we will become more like the risen and ascended Christ every day. The rising holy ones will remain under the radiant light of the living Christ all the time, growing in strength and power until no challenge is too great for them.

The Spirit of Holiness was the radiant white lightning breaking through the tomb and severing the chains. The Bible clearly tells us that Jesus Christ was raised from the dead "**with power according to the Spirit of Holiness**" **(see Romans 1:4)**. The resurrection power of God is inseparable from true holiness. The army that the Lord is raising up will be clothed with a manifestation of holiness and resurrection power that far outweighs what any previous generation experienced. We will soon discover that one of the primary reasons Christ shed His blood was to raise up this particular generation of holy people. A large percentage of the prophecies in the Bible were specifically intended for us.

The Urgency of this Hour

One of the primary reasons the Father has chosen to raise up this mighty army of "holy ones" now is because this is the hour when the world will need them the most. Mankind is about to face unprecedented turmoil. The coming shaking will threaten to shatter the complex global systems that man has built. However, this will be the greatest hour for those that the Lord has called to draw near to Him. We are entering a time of deepening darkness and rising light. Isaiah prophesied about the hour that is approaching:

Arise, shine, for your light has come, and the glory of the Lord rises upon you.
See, darkness covers the earth and thick darkness is over the peoples, but the Lord rises upon you and his glory appears over you.
Nations will come to your light, and kings to the brightness of your dawn (Isaiah 60:1-3 NIV).

In the same hour that the we see the "deep darkness over the people" becoming even deeper and darker, we will also see the radiance of God's glory shining brighter from the holy ones that He has called to bring restoration to the earth and to the heart of man. The Lord is clearly speaking to us today with His thundering voice: "arise and shine!" However, it does not stop there. Once we rise, then the glory of the Lord will continue to "rise upon us," growing brighter and more radiant with each passing day as we press in to know Him more.

Those who reject the Spirit have inadvertently chosen to remain bound in dead religion, complacency, and compromise. As a result, they will not have the power to disciple the nations as Jesus instructed us to do (see Matthew 28:19). This is because they have failed to become disciples themselves by rejecting the Spirit of Holiness—the specific Helper and Counselor that Jesus assigned to us when He ascended (see John 14:26). However, the Father is calling us right now to reach up, look up, and cry out for complete restoration. He is calling us to be so filled and clothed with the Spirit of Holiness that we truly become the **"new creation" (see II Corinthians 5:17)** we are called to be.

It is time for us to stop being satisfied with mere salvation. When Christ returns, believers who have invested their lives primarily in carnal pursuits **"will be saved—even though only as one escaping through the flames" (see I Corinthians 3:15 NIV).** Like the foolish virgins, they will have no light to bring with them when they go to meet the Bridegroom. When they appear before the judgment seat of Christ, all of the "wood, hay, and stubble" (see I Corinthians 3:12) of a life lived solely for carnal pleasure or to please other people will be revealed as meaningless. However, those who press in to find a deeper walk with the Lord will become more and more like Him with every passing day. Their desires will be united with God's desires and they will invest their lives in spiritual pursuits. These are the ones who will already be shining with radiant light when they meet the Bridegroom, for they trimmed and lit their lamps before He arrived. They will present to Him all of their "gold, silver, and costly stones"—the spiritual pursuits that they invested their lives in—and He will welcome them into His eternal kingdom.

SMALL GROUP DISCUSSION QUESTIONS

<u>Foundation Scripture One: Read Ephesians 5:8-14</u>

1. What does it mean for us to become "children of the light?"

2. How should we expect God's light to impact our own lives and spheres of influence as the next move of God unfolds?

3. What kind of fruit should we look for from our encounters with the light of Christ?

4. Invite members of the group to testify about when they first "awakened" to Christ's reality and power.

<u>Foundation Scripture Two: Read Matthew 25:1-13</u>

5. At what time did the "wake-up call" come for the ten virgins?

6. What do you think the "midnight hour" will look like? What will be happening on the earth?

7. What kinds of lifestyle changes can we make now in order to "buy the oil" we will need to shine in dark times? (Note: In Scripture, oil symbolizes the presence, power, and anointing of the Holy Spirit.)

8. Close with a time of worship, prayer, or impartation. Ask the Father to fill every believer in the group with fresh oil.

The Spirit of Holiness 2

At the moment Christ was raised from the dead, His body was instantly healed and completely regenerated by an infusion of resurrection power. The only mark of suffering He kept were His scars—so these could be an eternal and material testimony of the redemption He purchased for us. This potent resurrection power announced Jesus Christ as the eternal Son of God. This resurrection power raised Him up to be seated with the Father, where He is now clothed in radiant eternal light and glory beyond our comprehension. Now, let us look more deeply into what actually happened when Christ was raised from the dead so we might see how to access His power for our own transformation.

Here is what the Bible tells us about the angels who attended Christ's resurrection, based on eyewitness accounts:

There was a violent earthquake, for an angel of the Lord came down from heaven and, going to the tomb, rolled back the stone and sat on it.
His appearance was like lightning, and his clothes were white as snow.
The guards were so afraid of him that they shook and became like dead men (Matthew 28:2-4 NIV).

Now Mary stood outside the tomb crying. As she wept, she bent over to look into the tomb

and saw two angels in white, seated where Jesus' body had been, one at the head and the other at the foot (John 20:11-12 NIV).

The two angels who attended Christ's resurrection had an appearance **"like lightning"** and clothes as **"white as snow."** They were clothed in so much power and glory that the burly Roman soldiers who guarded the tomb shook and fell to the ground like dead men as soon as they saw them—despite the fact they could be executed for dereliction of duty. However, these angels were merely attending this event as heralds and witnesses. The person that actually raised Christ from the dead is infinitely more powerful than these two angels clothed with lightning. But who was this mysterious "third person?" Paul explains the mystery of who raised Christ from the dead:

Paul, a bondservant of Jesus Christ, called to be an apostle, separated to the gospel of God

which He promised before through His prophets in the Holy Scriptures,

concerning His Son Jesus Christ our Lord, who was born of the seed of David according to the flesh,

and declared to be the Son of God with power according to the Spirit of Holiness, by the resurrection from the dead (Romans 1:1-4).

Christ was raised from the dead by the Spirit of Holiness. This Spirit of Holiness is the same beloved person of the Trinity that we normally refer to as the Holy Spirit. The Spirit of Holiness is not an attitude, a lifestyle, a feeling, or a system of moral behavior. The Spirit of Holiness is a person—the living Spirit of God Almighty. He was more than able to raise Christ from the dead because He also participated in the creation of all things.

As Christians, we have become overly familiar with His name but we know almost nothing about His true nature. In every place where we find the name "Holy Spirit" in the Bible, it may be exchanged for a much more potent name—the "Spirit of Holiness." We are accustomed to calling this infinitely powerful person the "Holy Spirit" and talking about how well we know Him. However, how well do we really know the Spirit of Holiness?

The Spirit of Holiness *is* the lightning of God. He is inseparable from the resurrection power of God. He is the radiant and pure white light that shines from Christ. He is the One who brooded over creation in the beginning. He is the One who gave life to the fish in the seas, the birds in the air, and the creatures on the ground at the exact moment the eternal Word spoke them into existence. When the mighty Father stretched out the heavens like a tent, when the Son declared that the sun, the moon, and the stars would be set in the sky, it was the Spirit of Holiness that set them spinning into orbit and blazing with magnificent power out of the depths of His own eternal flame. When man was formed out of the dust of the earth by the Father's own hands, he was given life and endowed with an eternal human spirit by the Spirit that breathed into his nostrils. The first man took his first breath only by the Spirit of Holiness.

The first man took his first breath only by the Spirit of Holiness.

It was the Spirit of Holiness that beckoned Abraham to consider the stars and called him to walk by faith. It was the Spirit of Holiness who called the prophets, anointed them with power, and brought them into the heavenly realms where Christ is seated eternally. He is the One who caused Sinai to shake and smoke like a furnace when Moses met with the Father. It was the Spirit of Holiness that anointed David as king to raise up the genetic line through which Christ would reign forever.

It was this same Spirit of Holiness that anointed Jesus Christ with power to heal the sick, raise the dead, and cast out demons. After He ascended, He imparted this same Spirit of Holiness to the apostles and to all who would believe in His name in the generations that followed. Throughout the history of mankind, anyone who has heard from the Lord or experienced any manifestation of Christ's redemption has done so only by the Spirit of Holiness.

What True "Holiness" Really Means

Most people use the word "holy" to describe something that is merely religious in nature and human in origin. In our common usage, the word "holy" simply places something in the category of religious culture, which is usually distinct from secular society. The reason most Christians today have abandoned the word "holy" altogether is because people now associate this word with lifeless religion and tradition. However, the word "holy" does not accurately describe sister Gertrude glaring at a new visitor who failed to put on a tie. The word has lost its true meaning almost entirely because we have tethered it to forms of religion with no real spiritual substance or power. The word "holy" actually describes profound spiritual realities that rise high above our shallow "religious" and "secular" categories.

The true definition for the word is found in the highest heaven, where God Almighty is seated eternally on a throne of blazing light and matchless glory. Before His throne are powerful spiritual beings—called Cherubim and Seraphim—who contemplate His nature continually. As they gaze into His radiant light, matchless glory, wisdom, and love, they find an even deeper and higher revelation of His perfection with every passing moment. This throne room is the nerve center, the power generator, from which all of the cosmos was created, is sustained, and will one day be restored to perfection. It is in response to this continual flow of revelation in the throne room that the Cherubim and Seraphim cry out day and night:

"Holy, holy, holy is the Lord Almighty; the whole earth is full of his glory" (Isaiah 6:3 NIV).

"Holy, Holy, Holy is the Lord God Almighty who was and is and is to come" (Revelation 4:8).

Based on these texts and many others, I define "holiness" as the supreme and spiritual nature of God Himself. Unless our religious systems are causing us to cry out "holy" day and night in response to the breathtaking revelation of God we are receiving, then they cannot properly be called "holy."

The word "holy" in Hebrew is *kadosh*, literally meaning, "separate" or "set apart."[1] However, I prefer the synonym "completely other," for all that is holy proceeds from the eternal heavenly realms where God is seated on His throne. That which is holy is set apart to serve heaven and has its origin in the eternal realms. For this reason, nothing can be called holy unless it fully belongs to the One seated on the throne. Likewise, nothing can remain holy unless it maintains this vital connection to the throne room, from which the sustaining life and redemptive judgments of God flow as an eternal river of fire. Holiness cannot be exerted in and through our lives unless we become properly connected to the Holy One seated on the throne in an eternal heavenly realm that is infinitely more "real" than the world we presently live in.

---

[1] See Brown-Driver-Briggs Hebrew Concordance.

A Higher Order

Anything that is holy is of a much higher order than things of human origin. This is why God tells us, **"For My thoughts are not your thoughts, nor are your ways My ways . . . For as the heavens are higher than the earth, so are My ways higher than your ways, and My thoughts higher than your thoughts"** (see Isaiah 55:8-9). When we learn to access God's higher ways and higher thoughts, then we begin to live a lifestyle of holiness that supersedes and transcends everything else.

The priests, apostles, and prophets of the Scriptures were called holy because they gave themselves to the service of the One on the throne in heaven. As such, they became vessels the Spirit of Holiness empowered to see, hear, and declare what was happening in heavenly places—including what the One on the throne was saying. They became conduits through which God's hidden mysteries could be openly revealed to men.

Our generation is about to see a dramatic surge of spiritual holiness that fully captivates our hearts and minds, deeply rooting us in heaven's fiery delights. The end result of this move of God will be a much deeper commitment to the Spirit of Holiness. We will find a higher and deeper walk with God where we are literally "lifted up" and "hidden" in Christ all the time. Paul explains how to find this deeper walk:

> **Since, then, you have been raised with Christ, set your hearts on things above, where Christ is seated at the right hand of God**
> **Set your minds on things above, not on earthly things.**
> **For you died, and your life is now hidden with Christ in God.**
> **When Christ, who is your life, appears, then you also will appear with Him in glory (Colossians 3:1-4 NIV).**

Spiritual holiness will give us a heavenly perspective. We will learn to live with our eyes fixed on heaven. We will learn to fix our eyes on the glorified Christ so completely that we begin to reflect His divine nature. Only this higher perspective can free us from the chains—our carnal tendencies, temptations, and fears—that keep us earth-bound. If we can learn to cultivate this perspective all the time, then our core nature will begin to change because what we behold has changed. Instead of living in chains, we will become children of the light who walk in God's light all the time.

Small Group Discussion Questions

Foundation Scripture One: Read John 20:24-31

1. Dismantling heresy: Clearly explain to the group the importance of Christ's resurrection. Jesus was not raised only in Spirit, but in body so that all who trust in Him may receive resurrected and glorified bodies when He returns in power and glory.

2. Why was it important that the apostles were eyewitnesses of the resurrected Christ? What kind of legacy does this leave for us?

3. Read I John 1:1-4.

4. In this text, what does John say about the purpose of the apostles' close relationship with the living Christ?

Foundation Scripture Two: Read Colossians 3:1-4

5. According to the Scriptures, where are we positioned in relationship to Jesus Christ?

6. What can we do now to tap into the reality of being "hidden with God in Christ?"

7. What spiritual gifts or disciplines are most useful in helping us to shift our perspective from "earthly things" to "heavenly things"?

8. Give an opportunity for repentance to anyone afflicted with fear or anxiety because they have focused on "earthly things" more than "heavenly things." Then impart new hope, vision, and faith with words of prophetic encouragement.

Rediscovering Holiness 3

At the turn of the millennium, Bob Jones had a prophetic experience in which the Lord took him to "Satan's trophy room" to see all the things the powers of darkness had stolen from the body of Christ. The most treasured object in the enemy's possession was the "banner of holiness."[2] This banner was emblazoned with the Word of the Lord from Leviticus:

> "You shall be holy, for I the Lord your God am holy" (Leviticus 19:2).

Of all the things stolen from the church, Bob considered holiness to be the most significant. In his prophetic experience, he explained that "all hell broke loose" when he took this banner back. In Bob's revelation, he also noticed that the Scripture on the banner was written in a strange ancient language. He wrote down the characters he saw, which were later confirmed by others to be an ancient Semitic language predating modern Hebrew.

The most obvious message from Bob's revelation is that the Father wants to restore us to become a holy people. However,

---

2 See *You are My Friend*, by Bob Jones and Pastor Seung Woo Byun, pgs.110-112.

there are some other important truths hidden here. The revelation that "holiness" was stolen implies more than the fact that many Christians are backslidden or living in sin. The reality is that very few of us have a biblical understanding of real holiness—and even fewer know how to actually be holy in practical terms. We have not only lost our own embodiment of holiness, we have lost the concept altogether. However, the Bible makes it clear that holiness will be one of the primary characteristics marking God's people in the last days. It is time for us to begin rediscovering what holiness means so that we can learn to be the holy people that God has called us to become.

The other hidden message in Bob's revelation is that true holiness will be devastating to the enemy's work. The reason the banner of holiness was "Satan's most treasured possession" is because the Bible tells us that only holy people will have the authority to rule and reign on the earth. Daniel prophesied about us:

But the holy people of the Most High will receive the kingdom and will possess it forever—yes, for ever and ever (Daniel 7:18 NIV).

The radiant light that will dethrone the powers of darkness and strip them of power will shine from the faces of holy people. Daniel describes these rising holy ones:

Those who are wise will shine like the brightness of the heavens, and those who lead many to righteousness, like the stars for ever and ever (Daniel 12:3 NIV).

Throughout his prophetic book, Daniel describes the end times as a struggle between holy people and the powers of darkness. It is tempting to try to discern the specific interpretation of every event that Daniel prophesied, especially when so much of what the Lord spoke through him has already been fulfilled with perfect accuracy. However, this is a fruitless pursuit unless we first learn to actually be the holy people he referred to.

Civil Authority and Spiritual Authority

We live in an era when biblical morality is questioned by the majority of Americans. Abortion and gay marriage are currently legal in all fifty states. Pornography has become a paralyzing addiction throughout our society, including among many believers. Psychedelic drugs and casual sex have been normalized as "rites of passage" for teenagers to experiment with on their way to adulthood. We are surrounded by a constant barrage of television and internet programs that promote perversion, occult activity, and instant gratification.

One important aspect of holiness is that we must stand firm on important moral issues. The U.S. Constitution makes it clear that we have the freedom to live by our religious convictions, speak out on any political issue, and vote according to our conscience. We also have the liberty to boycott corporations or media outlets that violate our convictions. However, the First Amendment right to voice our dissent, our right to vote for candidates that embrace biblical morality, and our right to boycott companies that promote immorality are all expressions of our civil authority.

Most evangelical and charismatic churches in America have defined holiness in strictly moral terms and have used civil authority as their primary weapon to combat increasing lawlessness, perversity, and wickedness in our society. We have identified where biblical morality is being undermined, and we have used political and economic strategies to make our voices heard. Let me be clear: It is good to use our civil authority to speak out on moral issues. God will continue to raise up leaders who can teach us to use our civil authority much more effectively in the coming decades to stem the rising tide of immorality and lawlessness. However, our use of civil authority is a mere side effect of the kind of holiness that Daniel referred to.

Spiritual authority has much more weight than civil authority because it proceeds from the One seated on the throne in heaven.

Real holiness will always bear the fruit of moral behavior in our lives, just as a good tree always bears good fruit. However, the roots of true holiness reach much deeper than moral behavior. Its power goes far beyond expressions of mere civil authority. Holiness carries a spiritual depth and power that we have yet to fully discover or embody. Once the golden roots of holiness grow in our heart and mind, we will become a people who abide in the presence of God all the time, carrying a spiritual authority that only His intimate friendship can bring.

Spiritual authority has much more weight than civil authority because it proceeds from the One seated on the throne in heaven. Civil authority can voice dissent, but spiritual authority brings conviction, repentance, and restoration. Civil authority can mobilize thousands of people in a righteous cause, but spiritual authority will mobilize thousands of angels to clear the way for the kingdom to come with signs and wonders following. We must learn to exercise both kinds of authority in order to fulfill God's purpose for our generation. However, only a spiritual holiness, which extends beyond simple morality and changes our core nature, will give us the spiritual authority needed to overcome in times of rising darkness.

Jesus warned that wickedness will increase as we approach the end of the age because **"the love of most will grow cold"** (see Matthew 24:12 NIV). As we approach more perilous times, we need more powerful weapons in our arsenal. Currently, we have a shallow definition of holiness. We inspect the fruit of moral behavior in our own lives and others, but we do not let the golden roots of holiness grow deeply in our lives. Our lives look clean from the outside, but inside we are still unpruned. We strive to do and say the right things, but we lack the depth of love and weight of authority that comes only from walking with the Holy One. As we move forward, let us continue to stand for righteousness and use our civil authority effectively. Yet, the time has come to deepen our walk until the source of all holiness takes root and grows inside of us.

Shallow Forms of Holiness

Two perilous views of holiness have been widely taught in the body of Christ. Both doctrines are dangerous deceptions designed to hold us back from our true destiny. We must identify and defuse these ticking time bombs to avoid the destruction these may bring to our lives, churches, and communities. Each of these time bombs is perpetuated by those who "have a form of godliness, but deny its power" (see II Timothy 3:5). In each case, a different aspect of God's power is rejected.

The first ticking time bomb is legalism. This time bomb destroys our spiritual lives by reducing the Gospel to a list of moral "do's and don'ts." Legalism is deceptive because it appears to offer a biblical concept of morality. Those with a legalistic mindset might appear to be very holy people on the outside. However, inside they are miserable and oppressed. This is because legalism seeks to please God through human effort and striving while rejecting the Spirit's active ministry that truly sets us free. Legalism is easy to recognize because it cannot remove our broken nature, and it inhibits the work of God in us and through us.

In His rebuke to the Pharisees in Matthew 23, Jesus clearly condemns legalism and explains how it works to destroy our spiritual lives. Legalism leads us to believe that we are living holy lives, even as our "inner man" remains fallen and unregenerated. The reason I refer to legalism as a "ticking time bomb" is because legalism allows us to keep the most destructive parts of our fallen nature, such as pride, condemnation of ourselves and others, anger, and rejection. Instead of allowing the Spirit of God to remove our fallen nature and give us a new spiritual nature, we place a lid of religious restrictions upon ourselves in an attempt to suppress our true thoughts and feelings.

At some point, this ticking time bomb will explode and our true colors will show. This is why Jesus warned the Pharisees not to leave the "inside of the cup" unclean. Only the Holy Spirit can clean the inside of the cup so that it will not poison ourselves or others. Until we learn to yield to His real, tangible, and transformative work, then our hearts and minds will remain poisonous, regardless of how moral our lives may look.

Spiritualized Legalism

For believers who identify themselves as Pentecostal, Charismatic, or "Spirit-filled," it is tempting to assume that we cannot possibly fall into the trap of legalism. However, we are still susceptible to a snare I refer to as "spiritualized legalism." Those who fall into this trap may genuinely hear from the Lord and attempt to walk with Him, but deep inside they are still convinced that God can only love them if they "do enough stuff" for Him—including operating in the gifts of the Spirit.

The striving created by this performance mentality robs us of the deep sense of rest, peace, and perfect love that serve as foundations for the upward journey in God. It is impossible to move forward in our spiritual lives until we truly learn to love and be loved by God, for the love of Christ is the antidote that cures the most broken places in our fallen nature. The deep sense of peace and rest that comes by recognizing that Christ's sacrifice was sufficient to redeem us, justify us, and sanctify us is the crucial foundation that must be established in our lives before moving forward. This is why Paul wrote:

There remains, then, a Sabbath-rest for the people of God;
for anyone who enters God's rest also rests from their works, just as God did from his.
Let us, therefore, make every effort to enter that rest, so that no one will perish by following their example of disobedience (Hebrews 4:9-11 NIV).

Legalism masquerades as a form of obedience to God when it is actually a form of disobedience to Him. We will know that we have abandoned legalism and all of its forms when we abide continually in the overwhelming peace that comes by resting our faith on what Christ accomplished for us. However, this does not mean that we will accomplish nothing—when we find our rest in God, it allows Him to rest in us to a greater degree. God intends for us to become a holy people who are zealous and fully consecrated to Him. He desires for us to expand His kingdom in all the earth. However, we will quickly be worn out by the gifts of the Spirit operating through us if we are not first "rooted and established" in love, which Paul describes as **"the most excellent way"** (see I Corinthians 12:31 NIV). Consider how Paul prayed for the believers he discipled:

I pray that out of his glorious riches he may strengthen you with power through his Spirit in your inner being,
so that Christ may dwell in your hearts through faith. And I pray that you, being rooted and established in love,
may have power, together with all the Lord's holy people, to grasp how wide and long and high and deep is the love of Christ,
and to know this love that surpasses knowledge—that

you may be filled to the measure of all the fullness of God (Ephesians 3:16-19 NIV).

In this passage, Paul tells us that our "inner being" can be strengthened, rooted, and established in love. We can receive power to gaze into Christ's eyes and contemplate the depths of His love. Ultimately, the greatest use of our prophetic gift is not to prophesy over other people or even to intercede for them in private. The greatest use of the gift of prophecy is as an avenue to draw closer to the Lord until we encounter His deep love face-to-face. This is a concept I explore more fully in *Paths of Ever-Increasing Glory*. It is only possible to pursue this kind of relationship if we are fully aware that His presence is living and active in us.

Religion and Rebellion are Brothers

The other ticking time bomb in the church is lawlessness. Lawlessness is a rejection of moral behavior, often under the guise of "grace." In the body of Christ, lawlessness usually arises after legalism has already run its course. For example, most of the current trends and false doctrines in the body of Christ today are this current generation's overreaction to the previous generation's legalism. The emphasis on developing "seeker sensitive" churches over the last few decades was meant to remedy the problems caused by dead religion. Likewise, erroneous "hyper grace" teachings are meant to minister to those wounded by the teachings of legalistic religion.

The problem is that we have simply replaced legalistic religion with a more comfortable and libertarian religious culture. I have nothing against lattes in the lobby or flip-flops on a preacher. The problem is that many churches have gone so far down this path that they are beginning to follow the world in abandoning moral absolutes. Many believers are now offered an inferior concept of grace that accepts the overwhelming grace and mercy of God as a concept, but does not call us to embody holiness or change our nature in any way. These trends prove that the ticking time bomb of legalism has already exploded. The powerless and watered-down religious culture of many modern churches is simply part of the wreckage.

Current libertarian trends in the body of Christ lead to the same end result as legalism. Believers are ultimately left in a fallen state, bound and gagged by a spirit of religion. Legalism and lawlessness are brothers with the shared end goal of robbing us of our full inheritance as believers.

A Tale of Two Sons

The best illustration for these two perils is Christ's parable of the prodigal son (see Luke 15:11-32). In this parable, the elder brother was a religious legalist out "working in the fields" all day and every day. He worked incredibly hard *for* the Father, but he never spent time *with* the Father. As a result, he was bitter, angry, and unable to enjoy life. If our lives are not infused with the overwhelming joy of the Father, then there is a good chance we have fallen into this trap already. We are not called to strive to please God apart from Him. We are called to first come to His table and then work *with Him* in the fields at the proper time.

The prodigal son does not represent a new convert, but rather someone who has known the Father just long enough to receive his inheritance. Having received the glorious inheritance of God's grace, he spent it all living a lifestyle of sin and rebellion far from the father's table. This parable doesn't simply address those who have left churches. It speaks to leaders and members of fellowships where holiness is no longer preached. There are many believers who will be "saved, but only as one escaping through the flames" (see I Corinthians 3:15) because they are investing their lives entirely in carnal pursuits.

Religion and rebellion are based on the same performance mentality. Religion and rebellion both define holiness in shallow terms, creating a distinct religious culture while denying the real and tangible power of the Gospel to transform us. In this sense, legalistic religion and hyper-grace versions of Christianity are both false gospels designed to keep us from discovering the true power of what Christ accomplished through His death and resurrection. The father wanted both sons to eat at his table.

Though there are two pitfalls here, there is only one solution. Intimate fellowship with the Father is the cure for both religious legalism and lawlessness. The only path to become holy is to walk with the Holy One daily until His nature influences every aspect of our being.

Spiritual Holiness

Stand at the crossroads and look; ask for the ancient paths, ask where the good way is, and walk in it, and you will find rest for your souls (see Jeremiah 6:16 NIV).

The path of holiness is not merely a "middle ground" between legalism and lawlessness. The path of holiness supersedes and transcends everything else. Legalism and lawlessness are aspects of religious systems that man created while the path of holiness is the "ancient path" of spiritual ascent that allows us to abide in the Lord continually (see Isaiah 35:8).

Christians stand at a crossroads today. The body of Christ will either be completely transformed in our generation or it will cease to exist. Those who advocate a more libertarian gospel have tried to transform the body of Christ so that it will continue to exist. Their intentions have been good. However, the false teachings and shallow spirituality they promote are accelerating the demise of many churches. At this intersection, they have merely chosen a different human path which is decisively not the ancient and holy highway of spiritual ascent that the Bible describes.

In this book, I am attempting to clear the brush and brambles away from the entrance to the ancient path. The primary qualities of this ancient path are that it is holy, it is spiritual, and it will leave us utterly transformed and undone by the living Christ. However, it is not enough to find the entrance to this holy path. Once we have found the "good way," we must continually walk in it so that we may find "rest for our souls" (see Jeremiah 6:16).

We must first learn to completely disassociate holiness from the kind of wearying religious striving we are accustomed to. The ancient path laid out before us will allow our souls to find a quality of rest unavailable anywhere else. However, this rest will require a deliberate choice to walk with God each day. Jesus beckons us today:

"Come to me, all you who are weary and burdened, and I will give you rest.
"Take my yoke upon you and learn from me, for I am gentle and humble in heart, and you will find rest for your souls.
"For my yoke is easy and my burden is light" (Matthew 11:28-30 NIV).

We are not walking alone in our pursuit. Just as the disciples walked and talked with Christ on the road to Emmaus until "their hearts burned within them" (see Luke 24:32), real holiness is something that tends to sneak up on us when walking with Christ becomes our daily pursuit.

The reason we never have to grow weary in our pursuit of holiness is because we are yoked together with Christ. This is an unfair yoke—He is pulling all the weight. We simply come along for the ride by choosing to yield to Him on every matter.

Identifying His Holy Ones

In the Scriptures, it is often difficult to discern if the phrase "holy ones" refers to holy angels or holy people. The angels of the Lord are heavily involved in raising up holy people. Similarly, holy people are heavily involved in releasing angelic ministry when they consecrate themselves, pray, and inquire of the Lord. This is why you will never find a holy person not surrounded by angels. Holy angels and holy people are meant to work together as catalysts for bringing the kingdom of heaven to earth. Consider how Paul describes the kingdom:

But you have come to Mount Zion, to the heavenly Jerusalem, the city of the living God. You have come to thousands upon thousands of angels in joyful assembly,
to the church of the firstborn, whose names are written in heaven. You have come to God, the judge of all men, to the spirits of righteous men made perfect,
to Jesus the mediator of a new covenant, and to the sprinkled blood of Jesus that speaks a better word than the blood of Abel (Hebrews 12:22-24 NIV84).

Notice that Paul wrote, "**you have come**" in the past tense—we are already a part of this kingdom. We already have access to the "**heavenly Jerusalem**" by the Spirit. Then Paul describes the kingdom as a joyful gathering that includes both angels and people. He also describes two distinct groups of people—the "**church of the firstborn**" and the "**spirits of righteous men made perfect.**" The first group refers to the body of Christ on the earth while the second group refers to the cloud of witnesses that he describes in the beginning of the chapter.

While Paul does not use the phrase "holy ones" here, he describes the same assembly of holy beings that will accompany Christ at His return—the angels, the saints who are still alive, and the cloud of witnesses. Paul includes these three groups in his detailed description of the second coming of the Lord in I Thessalonians 4:13-18. Based on these texts, the phrase "holy ones" sometimes refers to a combination of all three of these groups—especially in reference to the day of the Lord. It is important to make these distinctions clear from Scripture because some prophetic passages are unclear on exactly who the "holy ones" are. For example, Jude quotes directly from Enoch's prophecy about the coming of the Lord:

"See, the Lord is coming with thousands upon thousands of His holy ones
"to judge everyone, and to convict all the ungodly of all the ungodly acts they have done in an ungodly way, and of all the harsh words ungodly sinners have spoken against him" (Jude 1:14-15 NIV84).

I interpret these multitudes of "holy ones" to include the three groups that I described: angels, believers who are still alive, and those who have fallen asleep in Him. These will all accompany the Lord at His return. As we look more deeply into the rise of the "holy ones" in Scripture, the coming of the kingdom, and the councils of holy ones in heaven, we must bear in mind that the "holy ones" often include both holy angels and holy people.

The "Holy Ones" as Angelic Heralds

There are some passages of Scripture where there is no doubt that the "holy ones" refer exclusively to angels. For example, Daniel prophesied:

"This decision is by the decree of the watchers, and the sentence by the word of the holy ones, in order that the living may know that the Most High rules in the kingdom of men, gives it to whomever He will, and sets over it the lowest of men" (Daniel 4:17).

In this passage, Daniel describes a prophetic decree declared exclusively by "the watchers," which here refers to holy watcher angels, not fallen angels. In this case, the phrase "holy ones" refers exclusively to high-level angelic messengers who sit in council with the Lord and declare what happens in His throne room. Likewise, Daniel explains that this revelation was given to him by **"a watcher, a holy one, coming down from heaven" (see Daniel 4:13)**. This phrase refers exclusively to an angel.

Based on this chapter of Daniel, it might be tempting to view the ministry of the holy angels as something untouchable, unreachable, and too high above us to even consider encountering. One of the remarkable things about the Book of Daniel, however, is that Daniel worked in tandem with the holy angels to bring high-level revelation to the earth. If Daniel did not have **"the Spirit of the Holy God in him" (see Daniel 4:18)**, then we might have never known what these watchers decreed. Daniel's life is a testimony that holy people and holy angels can work together to bring revelation from heaven to earth.

Daniel's exclusive references to the "holy ones" as angels leads us back to the discovery of holy people. Every holy angel described in the Bible was first encountered by a holy person. In most cases, the angelic visitations that we see in the Bible happened in the lives of people fully consecrated to God as priests, prophets, or simple saints dedicated to prayer. Ultimately, all of the revelations of holy angels in the Scriptures were handed to us by people who were also made holy. As such, all of the holy angels and holy people of the past constitute a "great assembly" that has served to declare what God is saying throughout human history (see Psalm 68:11).

The "Holy Ones" as Saints

As I discussed in the previous chapter, the Hebrew word for "holy" is *kadosh*, an adjective describing something specifically connected to God Himself. Something that is "holy" is not merely religious in nature—it is spiritual in nature and originates from the throne of the Holy One. Something that is truly holy is eternal and transcends all of man's systems—including his religious ones.

The Hebrew word for "holy ones" is *kedoshim*, which is simply the word *kadosh* conjugated as a plural noun. This word usually describes the people whose lives are consecrated to God without reservation. Many translations, such as the New King James Bible, prefer to translate the word *kedoshim* as "saints." However, the word "saints" does not carry the same meaning as *kedoshim*. We tend to think of saints as icons in a Catholic or Orthodox church, or the historic religious people that we celebrate. In contrast, the primary characteristic of the *kedoshim* is that they are made holy. This means that their lives are guided more by what goes on in heaven than what happens on earth.

We tend to think of the *kedoshim* as a small and isolated group that was exclusive from the rest of the nation. For example, the priests were called to be "holy unto the Lord" and interceded on behalf of the rest of Israel. The prophets were uniquely anointed and set apart so that they could speak God's words to the nation. However, it was never God's intention for only a minority of the people to be holy.

The Mystery of the "Holy Nation"

All of Israel was called to be a **"holy nation" (see Exodus 19:6)**. The Lord came down on Sinai with the same magnitude of glory that surrounds Him in heaven and told Moses:

Speak to the entire assembly of Israel and say to them: "Be holy because I, the Lord your God, am holy" (Leviticus 19:2 NIV).

This verse reveals that the Lord wanted every man, woman, and child in Israel to become a vessel through which heavenly realities would be seen, heard, and declared. He wanted every person to belong to the One on the throne. The problem was that they rejected the voice of the Lord and did not want to encounter His glory directly. Consider what happened on Mount Sinai when Moses met with God:

When the people saw the thunder and lightning and heard the trumpet and saw the mountain in smoke, they trembled with fear. They stayed at a distance
and said to Moses, "Speak to us yourself and we will listen. But do not have God speak to us or we will die."
Moses said to the people, "Do not be afraid. God has come to test you, so that the fear of God will be with you to keep you from sinning."
The people remained at a distance, while Moses approached the thick darkness where God was (Exodus 20:18-21 NIV).

Moses saw God's glory and spoke with Him face-to-face until the glory of God radiated from him. God offered His intimate friendship to all of Israel, but they rejected the holiness that God offered. They declined the opportunity to meet with Him face-to-face and chose to "remain at a distance." As a result of distancing themselves from the Father's glory, they were left only with the Law, a mere shadow of what they were meant to become.

We see an even higher revelation of God's desire for Israel when He refers to this holy nation as His bride. As Christians, we usually think about the Old Covenant as an unmitigated disaster or a failed experiment. Many theologians in the past have reflected on Israel's epic failures and assigned her to the dustbin of history. However, here is how the Lord views ancient Israel:

"I remember the devotion of your youth, how as a bride you loved me and followed me through the wilderness,

through a land not sown.
"Israel was holy to the Lord, the first fruits of his harvest" (Jeremiah 2:2-3 NIV).

This is the language of a nostalgic lover longing for His bride to return to Him. God's holiness encompasses more than His creative power or the proceedings in His throne room—His holiness carries the essence of a love that transcends and supersedes all other forms of love. This is why the ancient Jewish call to prayer features abandoned love as its centerpiece:

Hear, O Israel: The Lord our God, the Lord is one.
Love the Lord your God with all your heart and with all your soul and with all your strength (Deuteronomy 6:4-5 NIV).

As a Jew, Jesus grew up hearing this call to prayer every morning and evening. He was also present as the eternal Living Word when these instructions were first given to Moses on the mountain. This call to love God with full abandonment is what Jesus considered to be the most important of all of the commandments given on the burning mountain:

Hearing that Jesus had silenced the Sadducees, the Pharisees got together.
One of them, an expert in the law, tested him with this question:
"Teacher, which is the greatest commandment in the Law?"
Jesus replied: "Love the Lord your God with all your heart and with all your soul and with all your mind."
This is the first and greatest commandment.
And the second is like it: "Love your neighbor as yourself. "
All the Law and the Prophets hang on these two commandments (Matthew 22:34-40 NIV).

Love is the foundation to becoming a holy people. However, we cannot learn to abide in love towards God or our fellow man unless we develop the attitude of a young bride. In this sense, the law was a marriage contract between God and Israel, the holy nation. If you boil down all of the commandments given to them, He was basically saying: *"Don't cheat on Me. If you really have learned to love Me with your whole being, then this will be the natural fruit in your life."*

All that the Lord wants is a bride who will love Him and be fully dedicated to Him. He wants someone who can share in His glory, participate in His inexpressible joy, and carry the limitless depths of His love. Those who celebrate the Law and reject Christ are like a young bride spending her wedding night alone reading over the prenuptial agreement. They have rejected the intimate communion our Bridegroom desires of us. Those who reject intimacy with God will remain spiritually barren, for all of the pleasure and fruitfulness of a spiritual life originates with our "common-union" with Him.

Paul made it clear that the Law was merely the **"tutor to bring us to Christ, that we might be justified by faith"** (see Galatians 3:24). Throughout all of history, there was only one man who kept the marriage contract in full. There was only one man who never turned His heart or mind away from abandoned love to the Father. There was only one man who lived His life in perfect synchronicity with the Spirit of Holiness, being endowed with the fullness of His wisdom, love, and power. It is only through faith in Christ that we are now saved. However, the ancient mystery I am striving to bring forth into the full light of day is that God is presently restoring His holy nation to be the bride that He dreamed of from the beginning.

The New Jerusalem

When Israel was declared "holy to the Lord," she was also introduced as the "first fruits of His harvest" (see Jeremiah 2:2-3). The multitudes that God will redeem from every nation will also follow this pattern of becoming "holy to the Lord." The New Jerusalem is nothing less than the complete restoration and expansion of the holy nation that God has always desired to raise up as a blessing to all other nations. It encompasses the fulfillment of every one of the Father's promises concerning the restoration of mankind and the redemption of the earth from the curse of the Fall. The New Jerusalem is not a replacement for ancient Israel, but the resurrection and glorification of Israel so that every one of His ancient promises to His young bride might be proven accurate. This restoration is so grand that it now encompasses every Gentile who desires to become a part of it, including you and me.

When we examine the mystery of the New Jerusalem, we find that it describes a people, a city, and a nation made completely holy. This city is so connected to what is happening in heaven that it brings God's throne down to the earth. This city is the supreme accomplishment of all that God has desired—the restoration of His bride to a place of complete intimacy. Here is how the Scriptures describe this restoration:

> Then I saw a "new heaven and a new earth," for the first heaven and the first earth had passed away, and there was no longer any sea.
> I saw the Holy City, the new Jerusalem, coming down out of heaven from God, prepared as a bride beautifully dressed for her husband.
> And I heard a loud voice from the throne saying, "Now the dwelling of God is with men, and he will live with them. They will be his people, and God himself will be with them and be their God.
> "He will wipe every tear from their eyes. There will be no more death or mourning or crying or pain, for the old order of things has passed away" (Revelation 21:1-4 NIV).

Here we see the core purpose of the Spirit of Holiness working in our lives—to bring us into a holiness so complete that we can properly be called God's bride. This holiness is spiritual in nature—it will allow us to become so connected to the throne room that we actually became vessels through which God's throne is established on the earth, so that the reality of heaven floods into the material realm and removes the curse of the Fall. This holiness certainly includes righteous moral behavior, but this is only one small aspect of the kind of spiritual holiness that God is calling us into. Ultimately, righteousness will simply be a side effect of the deeper communion with God that we will experience when we learn to "set our minds on things above" (see Colossians 3:2). This is a city where everyone has learned to live in perfect communion with God all the time.

Revelation 21 and 22 describe what the complete fulfillment of the great commission looks like. We cannot say that we have successfully discipled the nations until they have each been fully grafted into the one holy nation, having the throne of God fully established in their midst and the curse of the Fall fully removed from them. We cannot say that our job is complete until we have built a dwelling for the Lord in the midst of a people made holy—a true *kedoshim*. We cannot say that we have succeeded until we have established a gateway to heaven through which the river of fire that flows from the Ancient of Days is given free reign to flow through the earth, displace the kingdom of darkness, and restore the heart of man.

SMALL GROUP DISCUSSION QUESTIONS

Analytical Questions:

1. How is spiritual authority different than civil authority?

2. How can we use our civil authority to have a positive and redemptive influence on our nation?

3. What can we do to exercise our spiritual authority more effectively—or at a "higher level?"

Foundation Scripture: Read Luke 15:11-31

4. What did the father offer to both of his sons?

5. Which son was more likely to eat at the father's table? Why was it easier for the rebellious son to find relationship with the father? What additional challenges did the older son face?

6. Read Matthew 11:25-30. What promises do Christ's words offer to those who feel burdened by legalism and dead religion?

7. What can we do individually to "enter His rest" and "take His yoke" upon us?

8. As the great harvest of souls unfolds in the nation, what can we do to make this group a place of encounter with God, where people of any background may find refuge, hope, and healing?

When His Holy Ones Assemble

The Coming Mountain of the Lord 4

One of my favorite movies is *Deep Impact* (1998). This classic apocalyptic movie portrays a massive asteroid, which will soon strike earth and transform life as we know it. The movie's promotional poster carried the potent words: *"Heaven and earth are about to collide."* In this movie, all of society is shaken by the grave realization that a large stone from the heavens is about to "deeply impact" the earth.

The coming kingdom of God is going to have a far greater impact on the earth than any asteroid ever could. For when the holy ones truly arise, the kingdom of God will advance with such ferocity that all of man's kingdoms and complex world systems will be shaken—until they are eventually removed. The Scriptures clearly lay out this unfolding reality. Furthermore, all of the signs indicate that we live in the times that the ancient prophets, from Enoch to John, spoke of with passion and longing.

In *Deep Impact*, two "scientists" discover the coming asteroid. One is an accomplished astronomer and the other is a young schoolboy who happened to look through his telescope at the right time. As I share what is about to unfold on the earth, I stand on the shoulders of seasoned prophets and accomplished Bible scholars who have far more expertise than I do. I just happened to be looking through the telescope at the right time. I wrote the following chapters because the weight of what I saw approaching is too great for me to keep silent.

For believers who have already looked carefully into the ancient mysteries of the Bible, these chapters will contain little that is new. However, many of the Bible's most important prophecies have been hidden from this current generation because they have not been preached from the pulpit. This message of the coming kingdom is one of the primary things that will raise up the generation of holy people that was prophesied. We cannot fully become who we are called to be until we first know what was written about us.

The Coming Mountain of the Lord

Imagine what would happen if an entire mountain was thrown from heaven towards earth. The results would be dramatic and catastrophic—the landscape of the whole world would change. Oceans and continents would be forever reshaped. The purpose of this book is not to predict that a literal asteroid will hit. Instead, my telescope is focused on something much more weighty and significant. My sights are set upon a spiritual mountain with the power to permanently "change the landscape" of human culture and understanding. This "coming mountain of the Lord" is the full expression of the kingdom of God on the earth. This "coming mountain" will reshape everything we know and believe, making way for the King of Glory to come and restore all things.

The Scriptures describe this mountain in great detail. Based on what I have read in the Scriptures and observed in the world around me, it is already being prepared for imminent impact. First, let us examine what Isaiah prophesied about the mountain of the Lord so that we can see what is supposed to happen there:

In the last days, the mountain of the Lord's temple will be established as the highest of the mountains; it will be exalted above the hills, and all nations will stream to it.

Many peoples will come and say, "Come, let us go up to the mountain of the Lord, to the temple of the God of Jacob. He will teach us his ways, so that we may walk in his paths." The law will go out from Zion, the word of the Lord from Jerusalem.

He will judge between the nations and will settle disputes for many peoples. They will beat their swords into plowshares and their spears into pruning hooks. Nation will not take up sword against nation, nor will they train for war anymore.

Come, descendants of Jacob, let us walk in the light of the Lord (Isaiah 2:2-5 NIV).

The mountain of the Lord is the place where the Lord's temple is established—the place where the full weight and radiance of His glory will rest. In the last days, this temple will be established so fully in the earth that people from every nation will cry out, **"Come, let us go up to the mountain of the Lord."**

On one level, this chapter prophesies the restoration of Israel and the temple mount, for the Scriptures clearly indicate that the Lord will restore His temple there—either now or in the age to come. However, the mountain of the Lord also speaks of a greater reality—the increase and establishment of the kingdom of God on earth. At some point, the kingdom of God will be a **"established as the highest of mountains"** so that **"all nations will stream to it."** The government of God being established in the earth will soon become much more significant and influential than any human government.

The mountain of the Lord is the only place where God will be able to **"teach us his ways, so that we may walk in his paths."** It is the only place where we may learn to reconcile God with man. It is also the only place where nations and ethnicities can be reconciled to the extent that centuries-old conflicts are resolved.

This is because it is the only place where we can truly learn to **"walk in the light of the Lord,"** which allows us to see other people and groups as He sees them.

The kingdom of God coming to the earth begins with the temple of the Lord being established. The current wave of worship, intercession, and prophetic declaration sweeping the global body of Christ will bear much greater fruit than anticipated. A temple for the Lord is being raised up, and His mountain is gradually growing, even as we see the mountains of man's kingdoms beginning to crack and crumble around the edges. In the coming decades, we will reach new levels of worship, intercession, and declaration that defy our previous understanding. We will see signs, wonders, and waves of harvest that defy our comprehension. This is because we are going to see the Lord of Glory begin to inhabit His body to a much greater degree. We will learn His ways, walk in His paths, and be guided by His light at all times. We will begin to accumulate enough wisdom to end conflicts between governments, religious groups, and ethnic groups.

The Mountain of the Lord as a House of Prayer

Isaiah also declares that as the mountain of the Lord is raised up, it will become a **"house of prayer for all nations"**:

"Also the sons of the foreigner who join themselves to the Lord, to serve Him, and to love the name of the Lord, to be His servants—everyone who keeps from defiling the Sabbath, and holds fast My covenant—
Even them I will bring to My holy mountain, and make them joyful in My house of prayer. Their burnt offerings and their sacrifices will be accepted on My altar; For My house shall be called a house of prayer for all nations."
The Lord God, who gathers the outcasts of Israel, says, "Yet I will gather to him others besides those who are gathered to him" (Isaiah 56:6-8).

Isaiah specifically tells us that Gentiles, which he calls "foreigners," will join themselves to the Lord, serve Him, and love His name. He tells us that their sacrifices will be accepted on His altar. He closes this passage with a promise that God Himself will "gather others" to His mountain. This refers to the Gentile nations being grafted into Israel through the promises of the New Covenant. As we see in the example of Christ clearing out the money changers, this is a vision He is very zealous about (see Matthew 21:12-13). As Christ turned over the tables of coins and accounting books, He quoted directly from Isaiah's prophecy.

Likewise, David prophesied specifically about all of the nations in the Middle East being included in the "others" who will be gathered to worship at Mount Zion:

He has founded his city on the holy mountain.
The Lord loves the gates of Zion more than all the other dwellings of Jacob.
Glorious things are said of you, city of God:
"I will record Rahab and Babylon among those who acknowledge me—Philistia too, and Tyre, along with Cush—and will say, 'This one was born in Zion.'"
Indeed, of Zion it will be said, "This one and that one were born in her, and the Most High himself will establish her."
The Lord will write in the register of the peoples: "This one was born in Zion."
As they make music they will sing, "All my fountains are in you" (Psalm 87:1-7 NIV).

If we simply modernize these names, it becomes clear that David is prophesying about the Middle East. Rahab is a poetic name for Egypt. Babylon is in modern Iraq. Philistine encompasses the Palestinian territories and beyond. Tyre and Cush refer to Syria and the nations of North Africa. Our focus on the negative prophecies in the Bible and the terrible events currently unfolding in this region has blinded us to the glorious promise of the harvest that will soon come out of it. Here, David prophesies that so many believers will arise from these nations that the Father will write in His register in heaven that these nations were born in Zion.

David also prophesies that a new sound in worship will come from this region as they acknowledge that **"all my fountains are in you."** As we survey the wreckage of the modern Middle East, David's prophecy seems unattainable. However, we have yet to see what is really possible when the Lord's mountain is raised up higher than any other mountain. At some point the nations of the Middle East will "beat their swords into plowshares and their spears into pruning hooks." This speaks of a transition among those who are being redeemed. Instead of making war against Israel, many will be taking up plowshares and pruning hooks, which speak of mutual peace and preparation for harvest.

The Mountain, the City, and the Name

Now let us consider how John described the mountain of the Lord:

One of the seven angels who had the seven bowls full of the seven last plagues came and said to me, "Come, I will show you the bride, the wife of the Lamb."
And he carried me away in the Spirit to a mountain great and high, and showed me the Holy City, Jerusalem, coming down out of heaven from God.
It shone with the glory of God, and its brilliance was like that of a very precious jewel, like a jasper, clear as crystal (Revelation 21:9-11 NIV).

Notice that John saw the New Jerusalem established on **"a mountain great and high."** The other prophets saw this same holy mountain. The difference is that John saw its spiritual nature and radiant glory with greater clarity because he operated under the New Covenant. John also described what happens there:

> I did not see a temple in the city, because the Lord God Almighty and the Lamb are its temple.
> The city does not need the sun or the moon to shine on it, for the glory of God gives it light, and the Lamb is its lamp.
> The nations will walk by its light, and the kings of the earth will bring their splendor into it.
> On no day will its gates ever be shut, for there will be no night there.
> The glory and honor of the nations will be brought into it.
> Nothing impure will ever enter it, nor will anyone who does what is shameful or deceitful, but only those whose names are written in the Lamb's book of life (Revelation 21:22-27 NIV).

John describes the temple—which is God Himself. He describes the light of the Lord—which is the light of the Lord Himself. And he describes the nations walking by its light. This is the same kind of reconciliation and restoration that the other prophetic voices declared.

The mountain's primary characteristic is that it is spiritual in nature and filled with holy people from all nations. It is inhabited and overshadowed by God Himself. The Father wants to unveil these essential characteristics of the kingdom of God to our generation. It is no accident that the Scriptures were closed with a full and open revelation of the coming mountain of the Lord—His fully prepared bride revealed on the earth. This is the fulfillment of all God has longed for through the ages. When He first fashioned Adam out of the dust of the earth, He was already looking forward to the bride that would one day arise from Adam and Eve's fallen descendants.

Paul's Description of the Mountain

Although not generally considered a prophet, Paul also describes this holy mountain in great detail. His text is worth repeating:

But you have come to Mount Zion, to the city of the living God, the heavenly Jerusalem. You have come to thousands upon thousands of angels in joyful assembly,

to the church of the firstborn, whose names are written in heaven. You have come to God, the Judge of all, to the spirits of the righteous made perfect,

to Jesus the mediator of a new covenant, and to the sprinkled blood that speaks a better word than the blood of Abel (Hebrews 12:22-24 NIV).

The most remarkable thing about this passage is that Paul describes "**the heavenly Jerusalem**" *before* John received the revelation of the New Jerusalem recorded in Revelation. Paul's description of "**the heavenly Jerusalem**" is similar to John's description because he focused on its distinct spiritual nature. I would not be surprised if Paul's inspiration for this passage came from the experience of being "caught up into the third heaven" (see II Corinthians 12:2) that he refers to in his letters. However, Paul does not end his letter with mere description. He gives us a stern warning and tells us why this mountain is important:

> *When God first fashioned Adam out of the dust of the earth, He was already looking forward to the bride that would one day arise from Adam and Eve's fallen descendants.*

See to it that you do not refuse him who speaks. If they did not escape when they refused him who warned them on earth, how much less will we, if we turn away from him who warns us from heaven?

At that time his voice shook the earth, but now he has promised, "Once more I will shake not only the earth but also the heavens."

The words "once more" indicate the removing of what can be shaken—that is, created things—so that what cannot be shaken may remain.

Therefore, since we are receiving a kingdom that cannot be shaken, let us be thankful, and so worship God acceptably with reverence and awe,

for our "God is a consuming fire" (Hebrews 12:25-29 NIV).

Just as John saw the establishment of the New Jerusalem after the seven bowls of God's wrath had been poured out on the earth, Paul associates the full unveiling of the "heavenly city" with a time when many things in this world will be severely shaken. These are clues leading us to the mystery of the coming mountain of the Lord. The mountain of His kingdom will deeply impact the earth at a time when the kingdoms of this world are disintegrating and passing away. The coming shaking will remove everything except the Lord's mountain that will increase with strength and stature until it fills the earth.

The Ferocity of the Coming Mountain

God gave King Nebuchadnezzar a dream of a massive idol representing the kingdoms of this world (see Daniel 2). When Daniel interpreted this dream, he presented an accurate prophetic outline for the series of governments that would rule from Nebuchadnezzar's time until the end of the age. The dream accurately predicted the progression and essential features of five successive human kingdoms: Babylon, the Medes and Persians, Greece,

Rome, and the weak and fractured governments and political alliances of today. Together, these kingdoms formed a massive idol, with each type of metal representing a different historic kingdom. Daniel also described a final mysterious kingdom that would arise:

> "You, O king, were watching; and behold, a great image! This great image, whose splendor was excellent, stood before you; and its form was awesome.
> This image's head was of fine gold, its chest and arms of silver, its belly and thighs of bronze,
> "its legs of iron, its feet partly of iron and partly of clay.
> "You watched while a stone was cut out without hands, which struck the image on its feet of iron and clay, and broke them in pieces.
> "Then the iron, the clay, the bronze, the silver, and the gold were crushed together, and became like chaff from the summer threshing floors; the wind carried them away so that no trace of them was found. And the stone that struck the image became a great mountain and filled the whole earth...
> "And in the days of these kings the God of heaven will set up a kingdom which shall never be destroyed; and the kingdom shall not be left to other people; it shall break in pieces and consume all these kingdoms, and it shall stand forever.
> "Inasmuch as you saw that the stone was cut out of the mountain without hands, and that it broke in pieces the iron, the bronze, the clay, the silver, and the gold—the great God has made known to the king what will come to pass after this. The dream is certain, and its interpretation is sure" (Daniel 2:31-35, 44-45).

Daniel describes the ultimate "deep impact"—the kingdom of God coming to earth. The stone that he describes is nothing less than the mountain of the Lord, the New Jerusalem, coming from heaven to displace all of man's kingdoms. The stone "**cut out without hands**" is the same "**city with foundations, whose**

architect and builder is God" (see Hebrews 11:10 NIV) that Abraham searched for. Here we find the prophetic promise that the kingdom of God will **"break in pieces and consume"** every other kingdom.

Daniel describes the same events that Isaiah described when he referred to the "mountain of the Lord's temple being established as the highest of the mountains" (see Isaiah 2:2). The prophets are unified in declaring that at some point, the governmental authority and dominion of the earth is going to be taken from our fallen and corrupt leaders and handed over to a holy people.

When considered together, the testimony of the prophets speak of more than the second coming of Christ. For the coming mountain is not Christ alone, but the city, the mountain, the holy people, and the holy angels that surround His throne. The stone coming with great ferocity to destroy and displace the kingdoms of this world is a kingdom, a heavenly city, and a holy people to which the curse of the Fall no longer applies.

SMALL GROUP DISCUSSION QUESTIONS

<u>Foundation Scripture One: Isaiah 2:2-5</u>

1. When do the Scriptures say the "mountain of the Lord's temple" will be established? Why does it say "last days" instead of "last day?"

2. What do you think it will look like when the Lord "teaches us His ways?"

3. How can we begin learning His ways right now?

4. Read verse four carefully. What does this verse promise about the end of war and the beginning of the great harvest of souls?

5. How can we encourage and assist every member of this group to "walk in the light of the Lord" each day?

<u>Foundation Scripture Two: Read Hebrews 12:18-24</u>

6. What makes the revelation of God's mountain under the New Covenant more complete than the revelation of God's mountain under the Law?

7. According to this Scripture, what kinds of spiritual realities do we have free access to under the New Covenant?

8. What are the benefits of seeing the mountain of God prophetically? Is seeing necessary in order to believe? Why or why not?

9. Activation: Set aside some time to "come to Zion" together as a group through worship, prayer, and waiting on the Lord for revelation.

A Tale of Two Cities

Those who object to the shaking and removal of man's kingdoms have not anticipated their true nature at the time of their removal. John described the end of the age as an epic struggle between two cities—or two spiritual realities. One is the New Jerusalem that I have already described. The other is called "Mystery Babylon," which represents all the kingdoms of man in their most evil state, completely possessed by the powers of darkness. The tale of these two cities in the Book of Revelation explains why the end of the age can simultaneously be the "best of times" and the "worst of times." We will see breathtaking restoration taking place in the heart of man as the New Jerusalem is revealed in these times. At the same time, we may see unparalleled wickedness and demonization happening in nations where Mystery Babylon takes root.

John's revelation of Babylon being removed and the New Jerusalem planted on the earth serves as a "second witness" to what Daniel prophesied. John and Daniel both speak of an epic showdown between the kingdoms of this world and the kingdom of God. The good news is that both prophets clearly indicate who will win. These two Scriptures, when taken together, should give us hope to keep pressing on, even when the heavenly bodies themselves are shaking.

One of the mysteries of Babylon is that it traces its roots back to the tower of Babel, the place where all of mankind defied God by trying to build a gateway to heaven apart from Him. A few generations after the flood, the people said to each other:

"Come, let us build ourselves a city, with a tower that reaches to the heavens, so that we may make a name for ourselves and not be scattered over the face of the earth" (Genesis 11:4 NIV).

Notice that Babel was built in defiance to God. It celebrated human accomplishment while shutting God out. It sought to "make a name" for the people while leaving no place for the Lord's name to rest. In this sense, Babel—or Babylon—is the exact opposite of the New Jerusalem. It is the ultimate expression of man's governance without God.

Nebuchadnezzar had this same spirit. He was concerned about the longevity of his own kingdom and his own name. This is why God gave him a series of terrifying dreams. He was humbled—first by having to rely on Daniel to receive the interpretation and later by losing his mind for a number of years until he acknowledged that God alone reigns supreme. After losing his mind so fully that he was eating grass and had not trimmed his hair or nails in a year, King Nebuchadnezzar finally declared:

"His dominion is an eternal dominion; his kingdom endures from generation to generation" (Daniel 4:34 NIV84).

Nebuchadnezzar was given a measure of unprecedented grace through this season of insanity. He was given the grace to humble himself before the Lord and acknowledge His Lordship. However, the "Mystery Babylon" that will emerge in the last days will have no such grace given to it. John prophesied:

"Fallen! Fallen is Babylon the Great! She has become a home for demons and a haunt for every evil spirit, a haunt for every unclean and detestable bird.

"For all the nations have drunk the maddening wine of her adulteries. The kings of the earth committed adultery with her, and the merchants of the earth grew rich from her excessive luxuries" (Revelation 18:2-3 NIV84).

Here we see that when Babylon fully matures, it will provide a resting place for all manner of evil. This is not merely figurative language. Some of the most significant world events of the last one hundred years involved governmental leaders who opened the door for demonic activity to flood the earth. Hitler, Stalin, and Mao Zedong are perhaps the best examples. Each of these leaders was obsessed with himself and his nation's "greatness" to the point that they became conduits through which demonic powers brought oppression and slaughter to countless lives. In each case, Jews or Christians were specifically targeted and slaughtered by the millions.

The reason that we can rejoice when the kingdoms of this world are shaken and removed is because the Bible tells us that they will exhibit a much higher level of demonization. John warns us that "Mystery Babylon" will be "drunk with the blood of the saints and the blood of those who bore testimony to Jesus" (see Revelation 17:6).

Today we stand in a unique moment of human history—we are standing just before the midnight hour. There are many nations and governments wavering in between the spiritual realities of these two cities. Some nations lean towards discipleship and consecration to the Lord. Other nations perpetuate great evil in the earth. As the midnight hour approaches, the Bible warns of a time when Mystery Babylon will reach its full maturity. At this time, we will see the full weight of evil expressed through human government. I will refrain from drawing conclusions about what this will look like or who will be in charge because these things have not been revealed to me. What has been revealed to me is that God is raising up a holy people who will walk in all the powers of the age to come. They will serve as shining lights in the midst of the darker times the Bible warns us about.

Coming Out of Babylon

The Bible gives us specific instructions concerning how to deal with Babylon effectively. This is the Father's clear command in the Book of Revelation:

"Come out of her, my people, so that you will not share in her sins, so that you will not receive any of her plagues;
"for her sins are piled up to heaven, and God has remembered her crimes" (Revelation 18:4-5 NIV84).

The first command is to remove ourselves from the system of spiritual bondage and oppression dominating this fallen world. However, the Bible also tells us how to come out of Babylon:

Awake, awake! Put on your strength, O Zion; Put on your beautiful garments, O Jerusalem, the holy city! For the uncircumcised and the unclean shall no longer come to you.
Shake yourself from the dust, arise; Sit down, O Jerusalem! Loose yourself from the bonds of your neck, O captive daughter of Zion! (Isaiah 52:1-2 NIV)

The Lord has made bare His holy arm In the eyes of all the nations; And all the ends of the earth shall see the salvation of our God.
Depart! Depart! Go out from there, touch no unclean thing; Go out from the midst of her, be clean, you who bear the vessels of the Lord.
For you shall not go out with haste, nor go by flight; For the Lord will go before you, and the God of Israel will be your rear guard (Isaiah 52:10-12 NIV).

In Scripture, the command to "awake" is often synonymous with a call to prayer. Our response to the rising evil should be to wake up spiritually and invest our lives in the heavenly city that God is building. We need to learn to pray much more effectively in order to overcome the darkness of the midnight hour. This is the only effective way to "come out" and "be separate" from the increasingly demonized systems of man. Let me be clear: This does not mean that Christians should react in fear or completely disengage from society. The same Scripture that commands us to **"go out from here and touch no unclean thing"** also promises that we **"will not go out with haste, nor go by flight"** because God will protect us every step of the way.

When we "rise and shine" spiritually as the holy ones we are called to be, then we successfully detach ourselves from the world system and connect ourselves to the New Jerusalem. As we make this spiritual transition, we also have the power to bring with us everyone in our sphere of influence and every thing under our authority. As a result, we can expect many nations to be discipled and many aspects of culture to be made holy as people wake up to the rising glory of the Lord.

The true children of God will have nothing to fear, even when the earth and the heavenly bodies are shaking. As the stars are falling and the beasts are rising out of the sea, even as saints are martyred for their faith, we will be clothed every morning with increasing strength, rising light, and greater glory. As we depart from the spiritual bondage of this world, we will put on the "garments of splendor" that will cause demonic forces to flee from us in terror.

Freedom to Hear from the Lord

We need to give people the freedom to hear from the Lord and obey Him, even if their instructions are different. For example, some leaders in the body of Christ, such as Lance

Wallnau, Johnny Enlow, and Dave Yarnes have described a "seven mountain mandate." These leaders have laid out a clear vision for believers to bring the kingdom of God into the "mountains" of arts and entertainment, business, education, family, government, media, and religion in the last days. This "seven mountain mandate vision" provides a clear structure for discipling the nations and "rising and shining" in dark times. This remarkably aggressive vision calls believers to stand and take new ground instead of shrinking back and surrendering our culture to the powers of darkness.

Others, such as Jim Bakker, John Paul Jackson, and Rabbi Jonathan Cahn have spoken of increasing judgment and the need to prepare for unprecedented natural disasters, rising persecution, or other "last days" events. They have emphasized the importance of personal preparedness, both as a means of self-preservation and as a tool for ministering to others. From this perspective, there might not be many mountains left to take after the dust settles.

We do not need to "choose sides." Instead, we need to see how the different messages being preached fit like puzzle pieces, forming a bigger picture of the rising glory and severe shaking about to unfold. At this time, some are being promoted to high levels of government authority or are learning to impact our culture with fresh creative vision. Others are buying cabins in the mountains filled with shelf-stable provisions. We each need to seek the Lord and hear from Him for ourselves.

Some may be called to be like Noah, who was boarded up alone in the ark with his family for self-preservation as judgment fell around him. This can be a very righteous choice, for God may be calling some to hide away so that He may save a remnant for Himself in the darkest regions of the earth. Others may be called to be like Joseph, who rose to the highest level of authority so that he could minister to multitudes in a time of famine.

We must grant freedom to believers to gravitate to whichever perspective they are being led to. For at some point, the Josephs may need the Noahs—or the other way around.

The Seal of God—The Ultimate "Prep Item"

The best kind of preparedness is drawing closer to the Lord until we are hearing from Him, abiding in Him, and walking with Him daily. This is why I wrote a book about holiness instead of a book about prepping. In Revelation 7, John saw that angels were "holding back" the winds of adversity until God's servants were given His seal:

> After this I saw four angels standing at the four corners of the earth, holding back the four winds of the earth to prevent any wind from blowing on the land or on the sea or on any tree.
> Then I saw another angel coming up from the east, having the seal of the living God. He called out in a loud voice to the four angels who had been given power to harm the land and the sea:
> "Do not harm the land or the sea or the trees until we put a seal on the foreheads of the servants of our God."
> Then I heard the number of those who were sealed; 144,000 from all the tribes of Israel" (Revelation 7:1-4 NIV84).

I have yet to hear a convincing or inspired interpretation of who the 144,000 are in this passage. Some have suggested that these are Messianic Jewish evangelists or a restored priesthood. Some smaller denominations and cults have even used this number to refer to their organization as having a role greater than the rest of the body of Christ. None of these interpretations ring true to me, and some are blatant heresy. Instead, I interpret 144,000 to be a spiritual number associated with the seal of God, just as the number 666 is a spiritual number associated with the mark of the beast. I believe that the seal of God is given to every believer who receives an anointing from the Holy Spirit. The reason I draw this conclusion is because Paul specifically tells us what the "seal of God" is in three different places:

> Now He who establishes us with you in Christ and has anointed us is God,
> who also has sealed us and given us the Spirit in our hearts as a guarantee (II Corinthians 1:21-22).

> In Him you also trusted, after you heard the word of truth, the gospel of your salvation; in whom also, having believed, you were sealed with the Holy Spirit of promise,
> who is the guarantee of our inheritance until the redemption of the purchased possession, to the praise of His glory (Ephesians 1:13-14).

> And do not grieve the Holy Spirit of God, by whom you were sealed for the day of redemption.
> Let all bitterness, wrath, anger, clamor, and evil speaking be put away from you, with all malice.
> And be kind to one another, tenderhearted, forgiving one another, even as God in Christ forgave you (Ephesians 4:30-32).

The first verse makes it clear that the seal of God is the anointing and presence of the Holy Spirit. The second verse makes it clear that this "seal" is available to anyone who places their faith in Christ. The third verse explains how we need to live so that we do not grieve the Spirit of Holiness, whose presence is the tangible mark that God has redeemed us.

I interpret this passage in Revelation to mean that God is literally holding back the winds of adversity until His people step into the level of holiness and spiritual ascent that He is calling them into. When you compare this text with Jesus' parable of the wise virgins, then the angels are basically assigned to give the wise virgins more time so that they can store up more oil before midnight falls. The question is, what are we doing with the extra time that we are being given?

The midnight hour does not merely represent natural disasters, wars, or increased immorality. The midnight hour speaks of a convergence of spiritual darkness that will make it hard to be anything but anxious, fearful, selfish, or deceived. It speaks of spiritual forces that are inherently oppressive and enslaving to the heart of mankind. Just as the New Jerusalem describes a convergence of all that is holy until it reaches full maturity, Mystery Babylon speaks of convergence of all that is unholy until it reaches a level of maturity demanding God's judgment. Most Christians have not anticipated how deep this darkness will be or how easy it will be to slip into it.

The reason that God holds these things back is because He desires a people who will walk in perfect peace, love, and wisdom when the rest of the world goes insane with anxiety. Some of the greatest kingdom works will come from people who have learned to abide in the peace and love of God in mundane day-to-day life. Those who live simple, peaceful, quiet, and godly lives will rise to shine radiantly in these times (see I Thessalonians 4:11).

What Does the "Seal of God" Look Like?

The seal of God is the literal, tangible presence of the Holy Spirit—or the Spirit of Holiness—resting upon our lives. The Bible gives us a clear picture of what this seal looks like and what it is meant to do:

"Make a plate of pure gold and engrave on it as on a seal: HOLY TO THE LORD.
"Fasten a blue cord to it to attach it to the turban; it is to be on the front of the turban.
"It will be on Aaron's forehead, and he will bear the guilt

involved in the sacred gifts the Israelites consecrate, whatever their gifts may be. It will be on Aaron's forehead continually so that they will be acceptable to the Lord" (Exodus 28:36-38 NIV).

Paul made it clear that the details of the Mosaic covenant were "shadows," or prophetic symbols, for the full reality of the kingdom that we inherit under the New Covenant. The fact that the Levitical priests had the words "Holy to the Lord" continually fastened to their forehead speaks of the Lord giving us a completely redeemed mind. Those who truly yield to the Spirit of Holiness in their thought-life will walk in a level of freedom beyond merely being free from sin or negative thoughts. We have the freedom to have a mind that is influenced by all that is holy. We have a mind that, as part of the "new creation" we become, has open access to heaven's vast expanses. We have a mind that can be dedicated daily to God until we become gateways for releasing all that is holy into the earth through worship, intercession, prophetic declaration, evangelism, and other acts of love.

> *Unless we train ourselves to yield to the work of the Spirit in this present time when the winds are held back, we will not be ready to stand and shine in the times of turmoil that are coming.*

Our legalism has trained our minds to resist holiness because we see it as primarily restrictive in nature. However, I see the primary purpose of this gold seal as one of protection. For in the times that are unfolding, we will desperately need our minds guarded from the influence of rising evil on the earth. Unless we train ourselves to yield to the work of the Spirit in this present time when the winds are held back, we will not be ready to stand and shine in the times of turmoil that are coming.

We need to seek the seal of holiness on all that we do. I have often asked the Lord what He thinks about a particular song, movie, or teaching I have heard. I have yet to hear the Lord tell me that He does not like something. What He tells me is that He does not recognize something. If what we do originates from heaven or is directed by the Spirit of the Lord, then it is holy to the Lord, even if it is not explicitly "religious" in nature. God recognizes what belongs to His kingdom. For this reason, business leaders, artists, politicians, or all manner of vocations can seek God's direction and blessing as they pursue their calling. If God says that the kingdom of God is going to "fill the earth," then we should not be surprised as He moves through every kind of vocation in every sector of our society. In many cases, God even works through those who we would not expect to produce something that He will recognize. Yet, anything that God did not originate is something that He does not recognize—unfortunately, this includes many of the religious structures, teachings, and songs produced simply to make a name for ourselves.

The unfortunate reality is that at the present moment, God does not recognize much of the body of Christ in the Western world because much of what is happening did not originate with Him. The good news is that this will quickly change as the next move of God unfolds. We will learn to fully consecrate ourselves to Him and yield our whole being and our pursuits to His Spirit of Holiness.

The Violent Advance of the Kingdom

Jesus said, **"And from the days of John the Baptist until now the kingdom of heaven suffers violence, and the violent take it by force"** (Matthew 11:12). In context, Jesus was talking about real persecution. He was speaking at a time when the kingdom of God still appeared as a small stone encompassing a small group of people. Mary and Joseph had to flee to Egypt in order to escape Jesus being slaughtered before His earthly ministry even began. Likewise, John the Baptist was beheaded shortly after Christ spoke these words. Jesus was speaking about the fierce opposition to His kingdom from the powers of darkness, which are often manifested in violent acts of persecution.

There is also a deeper reason why the powers of darkness—and the rulers of this world—would strive to stamp out the prophets in their infancy. When fully mature, the kingdom of God will displace their kingdoms, taking away their power, authority, and dominion. The spiritual rulers of this age will be toppled from their thrones by the decisive rise of a holy people.

Fire From the Altar of Incense

In Revelation 8, we see a clear picture of what it looks like when the kingdom of God displaces all other kingdoms:

Another angel, who had a golden censer, came and stood at the altar. He was given much incense to offer, together with the prayers of all the saints, on the golden altar before the throne.
The smoke of the incense, together with the prayers of the saints, went up before God from the angel's hand.
Then the angel took the censer, filled it with fire from the altar, and hurled it on the earth; and there came peals of thunder, rumblings, flashes of lightning, and an earthquake (Revelation 8:3-5 NIV).

The events in the chapters following this description include terrifying judgments announced with seven trumpets. At the last trumpet, we hear the words:

"The kingdom of the world has become the kingdom of our Lord and of His Christ, and he will reign forever and ever" (Revelation 11:15 NIV84).

The important thing to take away from these passages is that when the times of shaking come, it will be for the ultimate purpose of removing every kingdom that can be shaken and establishing the kingdom that cannot be shaken. We must strive to remember this when sudden destruction seems to strike the world around us. Man's systems are simply being removed to make room for something much better.

There is also something of even deeper significance to take from this passage. These judgments are released because the prayers of the holy ones, stored up through the ages, are finally released to impact the earth. Primarily, we are called to be priests who intercede on behalf of mankind, petitioning God for grace and mercy. However, at some point, God may call us to pray against unrighteous and oppressive systems, just as one would have been justified in praying for the toppling of the Nazi regime.

The Final Exodus

One of the best ways to understand the Book of Revelation is to read it alongside the story of the Exodus. Just as God's people suffered in oppressive slavery in Egypt, so the holy ones will contend against the Pharaohs of their times. The purpose of the plagues upon Egypt was so that God could demonstrate His wonders and liberate His people. He intentionally hardened Pharaoh's heart so that He would have the opportunity to show His strength. Likewise, God will allow the oppressive leaders that Revelation describes as "beasts" to arise and rule for a short season for the purpose of showing Himself strong. The plagues of Egypt could not touch the Israelites. Likewise, some of the most terrifying judgments of Revelation are forbidden from harming **"only those people who have the seal of God on their foreheads"** (see **Revelation 9:4 NIV**). God brought His people out of Egypt so that they could freely worship Him. Likewise, God will allow—and even orchestrate—the events Revelation describes for the end goal of establishing His eternal kingdom on earth.

The parallel goes even deeper. Just as two witnesses prophesied to Pharaoh at the time of the Exodus—Moses and Aaron—we see two witnesses arise in the end times with an unprecedented level of power and authority. I do not believe that the identity of the two witnesses has been fully revealed yet. This may even speak of a much larger group of people who serve the same kind of role that Moses and Aaron served at the time of the Exodus. At some point, the Lord will raise up leaders with the power and authority to disciple nations as He instructed.

God's servants will have His seal before these dark times arise. We have been given time to prepare, to draw near to God and consecrate ourselves as holy. God is going to raise up prophetic leaders who have the capacity to speak to the heavens, to the earth, and to the sea and see their declarations fulfilled. The two witnesses may be interpreted both as two literal prophets from the cloud of witnesses who guide our generation to maturity *and* as a prophetic symbol describing the prophetic generation they are working to raise up now.

When the children of Israel left Egypt, they were given vast treasure. The gold, silver, and costly stones they were given were used to construct a tabernacle where the Lord could dwell. Likewise, the treasure we will be given will be used to construct the heavenly city and tabernacle of the Father's design. The treasure that we are being given will be much greater than gold, silver, or precious gems. The Father is going to shake the kingdoms of the world violently until they finally release what the Father considers His greatest treasure: "**a great multitude from every tribe, tongue, and nation.**" This great harvest of souls is the "treasure" He will use to construct His eternal kingdom. Each "living stone" already has a place marked out for him somewhere in the New Jerusalem's vast and glorious landscape.

The end will not come until Babylon is successfully looted of the souls held captive by its darkness and deception. Our ultimate goal is to free as many people as possible from the darkness of this world and make them "children of the light." Then the Father can plant them in His eternal city. The best way for us to accomplish this task is not to march into Babylon with swords drawn, but to build the Kingdom of Light according to the Father's blueprints, not our own.

SMALL GROUP DISCUSSION QUESTIONS

Foundation Scripture One: Revelation 18:

Review: Mystery Babylon represents a "mature expression of evil" in the kingdoms of this world.

1. Who inhabits this city (verse 2)? What has happened to the people in this city? How or why did it happen?

2. What does the angel of God declare over this city (see verse 2, 16-17)? How is this declaration an encouragement for God's people?

3. What are God's instructions to His people concerning "Mystery Babylon?"

4. What is the best way to "come out" of the demonization of the fallen world around us? (Or to reference a popular movie, how can we "unplug from the Matrix?)

Foundation Scripture Two: Read Revelation 21 and 22:1-6

Review: The New Jerusalem represents a "mature expression of the kingdom of heaven" on earth.

5. Who inhabits this city? What has happened to the people in this city? How or why did it happen?

6. What does God declare over this city (verses 3-5)?

7. What are Christ's instructions to anyone who wants to begin "drinking" from the waters of Life (verse 6)?

8. What can we do individually to "connect" to spiritual Zion and live lives freed from the curse of sin and death?

9. How can we make this group an "embassy" of the kingdom of heaven, where weary sojourners can find refuge and restoration?

10. Provide an opportunity for repentance and seeking God. This is an opportunity to reject the world's influence and embrace the kingdom of heaven's advancement in our lives.

Ruling and Reigning 6

Some of the prophetic voices I trust predicted that in March of 2015, a significant earthquake would strike the West Coast of the United States. As an intercessor, I considered this to be an urgent matter for prayer. As I interceded for the West Coast while washing dishes in my kitchen, I felt a dramatic increase of the presence of the Lord in the room until I knew He was there. Then I began to pray prophetically:

"Father, don't let this matter be decided by the powers of darkness or the fallen ones. Don't let this matter be decided by the angels. Don't let this matter even be decided by the earth itself. Let this matter be decided by the holy ones that You are raising up to counsel together in this region."

As soon as the words "holy ones" escaped my lips, a remarkable thing happened. I heard a strange sound, like the shattering of crystal and a loud bang at the same time, right outside my kitchen window. At this same moment, the power went out in my house. My golden retriever starting barking frantically and my sons wondered what was going on. The power was restored about a minute later, and there was no natural explanation for what happened. I found nothing broken outside or inside the house to explain the bang or the sound of shattering crystal that I heard.

I believe what I experienced was a surge of spiritual power. The Father wanted to demonstrate to me that I had discovered an important matter on His heart: His desire to raise up a holy people that will counsel together and with Him. Many in the body of Christ have written about this topic recently. Most of those teaching about the "councils" and "counsel" of the Lord have focused on the heavenly places where angels, saints, and the Lord Himself meet together to decide what will happen on the earth.

The Heavenly Model

What the Lord desires to raise up on earth usually has a clear blueprint functioning in heaven. There are twenty-four elders seated on thrones around the Lord's throne for a reason. Nearly everything the Lord does on earth is decided first by His council in heaven. The clearest example of this is presented in Daniel 7, where Daniel describes the heavenly council of the Lord being set up for a regular business day:

"As I looked, thrones were set in place, and the Ancient of Days took his seat. His clothing was as white as snow; the hair of his head was white like wool. His throne was flaming with fire, and its wheels were all ablaze.
"A river of fire was flowing, coming out from before him. Thousands upon thousands attended him; ten thousand times ten thousand stood before him. The court was seated, and the books were opened" (Daniel 7:9-10 NIV).

Before we describe *what* is happening in the Lord's council, let us look at *who* is included there. First, we see that the Lord's throne is not the only throne present. There are also "thrones set in place" around Him, the ones who counsel together with the Lord in deciding what will happen next. The placement of the twenty-four elders on thrones around the Lord does not mean that they are assuming the place of God. It means that their authority is derived completely from His authority. Their decisions are rooted in His decisions. They all face Him, the wellspring of all wisdom and understanding, so that they can become the tributaries through which His wisdom flows out of the heavenly realms and into the earth.

We also see an assembly of multitudes surrounding this holy council. This is a vast body of holy ones that most likely includes all those who are part of God's kingdom—the assemblies of angels, the cloud of witnesses, and the church on earth who has learned to abide in heavenly places. Lastly, the Lord declares that court is in session and the books are opened.

The opening of the books is important because even the "Ancient of the Days" is constrained by what He has already written. Ultimately, His counsel is responsible for releasing the fulfillment of everything written in heaven before the world was made. For this reason, the counsel of the Lord is synonymous with open-book revelation. There is no matter hidden from the counsel of the Lord. He sees from the beginning to the end—and every detail in between—simultaneously. He sees every decision made, being made, and that will be made through history. He sees every event that has happened, is happening, and will happen as a single image. Theologians have words to describe these aspects of God's nature: He is eternal, reigning from outside the realm of time and space, and He is omniscient, with full knowledge of everything that is and will be. The mystery I am declaring is that the holy ones currently being raised up will begin to access the

The holy ones currently being raised up will begin to access the Lord's counsel in much deeper ways so that they can release it on the earth.

Lord's counsel in much deeper and fuller ways so that they can release it on the earth.

The Purpose of the Council

In his interpretation of this courtroom scene, the angel explaining this prophetic experience to Daniel specifically applies it to us:

"So he told me and gave me the interpretation of these things:
'The four great beasts are four kingdoms that will rise from the earth.
"But the saints of the Most High will receive the kingdom and will possess it forever—yes, forever and ever'" (see Daniel 7:16-18 NIV).

First, we must understand what the beasts are. A careful reading of Daniel 7 in context reveals that the reigning council of the Lord was in session for the purpose of dealing with these beasts. These beasts are simply prophetic symbols that speak of the successive kingdoms of man over human history, from ancient Babylon through to today's global systems. The "beastly" nature of these human kingdoms is a result of human wickedness and demonic influence.

The promise is that the river of fire proceeding from the Ancient of Days will strip these kingdoms of their authority and grant possession of the earth to His holy ones. In other words, this council is meeting to discuss what is already written about the transference of government from the kingdoms of this world to the holy ones. If this is really true, then we should begin looking to see what the government God is raising up on earth will look like. If we are simply "going up" to see what is happening in heaven, then we are only doing half of our job. We also have to bring heavenly blueprints back down to earth.

Only then can we become the rising kingdom and reigning priesthood the Father calls us to become (see Revelation 5:10).

Stewarding the Lord's Vineyard

> *"Take the words of Jesus and let them be the Supreme Court of the Gospel to you."*—John G. Lake

Some may consider this to be new theology, so let us return to the words of Jesus Christ who is the "supreme court" of doctrine. Jesus spoke to His disciples clearly about the restoration of all things:

> "I tell you the truth, at the renewal of all things, when the Son of Man sits on his glorious throne, you who have followed me will also sit on twelve thrones, judging the twelve drives of Israel.
>
> "And everyone who has left houses or brothers or sisters or father or mother or children or fields for my sake will receive a hundred times as much and will inherit eternal life.
>
> "But many who are first will be last, and many who are last will be first" (Matthew 19:28-30 NIV).

Here, Jesus makes it clear that He will grant unprecedented authority to His followers. He indicates that His twelve apostles will sit on twelve thrones and that everyone who followed Him will receive a hundred-fold restoration of what they left behind. However, the questions remain: How much authority are we called to carry in this life? How much restoration is possible?

These questions are answered by the parable that Jesus told immediately following this passage. In this parable, the workers of a vineyard are hired to tend the master's vineyard. At the end of the story, they are all paid the same amount for their service to the master, whether they worked for many hours or did not show up until the eleventh hour. The central message of this parable is the same as in the previous passage: "**So the last will be first, and the first will be last**" (Matthew 20:16 NIV).

The Master has entrusted His vineyard to us. He has also given us the authority and power to bring complete restoration, so that we bring the kingdom of heaven to earth. The questions we should be asking are not, "Where do we begin?" and "Why haven't we started yet?" Jesus' words show that we should be more concerned with doing the work of the kingdom than earning the honor that often follows that work. As any good manager, Jesus is not looking for people who want a great title. He is looking for those who faithfully obey and take care of what is entrusted to them.

Until He returns in power and glory, it is up to us to tend the Lord's vineyard. As long as God's people remain isolated, depressed, and alone, the vineyard entrusted to us will remain shriveled, fruitless, and in ruins. We must develop a new theology for ruling and reigning in holy council because this is the most biblical and effective way of managing everything the Lord entrusted to us when He ascended. The ultimate goal of establishing holy councils over regions of the earth is to present the Lord with a glorious bride and a fruitful vineyard. This kind of restoration can only happen when we lay hold of the unbreakable unity Jesus prayed we would have (see John 17).

There is also one very provocative interpretation of the parable of the vineyard. Immediately after telling the original twelve disciples that they will sit on twelve thrones at the restoration of all things, Jesus tells them "but the last shall be first...." The parable He shares explains that the payment will be the same for eleventh hour workers, or the last generation to steward the vineyard. I interpret this to mean that this final generation will receive a much greater revelation of authority than the early church walked in.

The Key of David

The restoration of all things is foreshadowed by the restoration that happened during David's reign. This is why the angel Gabriel told Mary:

"Do not be afraid, Mary; you have found favor with God.

"You will conceive and give birth to a son, and you are to call him Jesus.

"He will be great and will be called the Son of the Most High. The Lord God will give him the throne of his father David,

"and he will reign over Jacob's descendants forever; his kingdom will never end" (Luke 1:30-33 NIV).

We see two essential truths in Gabriel's message to Mary: Christ will be "given the throne of David" and "His kingdom will never end." If the King we serve will be seated on the throne of David that results in His kingdom never ending, then it seems worthwhile to see what was happening during David's reign.

Many of the Davidic blueprints that the Father is restoring in this hour are important keys opening doors for our generation to fulfill its destiny. This is why it is written:

I will place on his shoulder the key to the house of David; what he opens no one can shut, and what he shuts no one can open.

I will drive him like a peg into a firm place; he will become a seat of honor for the house of his father.

All the glory of his family will hang on him: its offspring and offshoots—all its lesser vessels, from the bowls to all the jars (Isaiah 22:22-24 NIV).

The living Christ cited this exact text and applied it to Himself when He spoke to Philadelphia, the faithful church:

"These are the words of him who is holy and true, who holds the key of David. What he opens no one can shut, and what he shuts no one can open.

"I know your deeds. See, I have placed before you an open door that no one can shut. I know that you have little strength, yet you have kept my word and have not denied my name" (see Revelation 3:7-8 NIV).

Here, Christ indicates that the promise Gabriel gave to Mary was fulfilled. He already has the throne of David and holds the key to His house. When my realtor gave me a set of five golden keys to my house, it signified that the property was now mine. These keys signified the transference of this property's authority and possession to me. Likewise, when the keys to the house of David are released to us, it signifies that we are being given a new level of authority to "reign on the earth" as "a kingdom and priests" (see Revelation 5:10).

In both texts describing the key of David that Christ now holds, we see that this key is associated with opening doors and closing doors. What are these "doors" being opened and closed? Jesus clarifies the matter. As soon as Peter acknowledged Christ as the Messiah, Jesus told him:

"Blessed are you, Simon son of Jonah, for this was not revealed to you by flesh and blood, but by my Father in heaven.

"And I tell you that you are Peter, and on this rock I will build my church, and the gates of Hades will not overcome it.

"I will give you the keys of the kingdom of heaven; whatever you bind on earth will be bound in heaven, and whatever you loose on earth will be loosed in heaven" (see Matthew 16:17-19 NIV).

The door that the keys of the kingdom shut is nothing less than the gates of hell. The door that the keys of the kingdom open is the gateway to heaven through which the New Jerusalem will descend. When we learn to function as a "kingdom and priests," then we will "reign on the earth." We will bind the powers of darkness until the gates of hell are shut in our region. Then we will loose the kingdom of God on earth until heavenly realities flood down into the earthly realm.

Throughout the last few decades, the body of Christ has been rediscovering the keys to the house of David. It is important to review what we have recently learned so that the new things God is revealing may be placed in proper context.

The Tabernacle of David

Many leaders in the body of Christ have taught extensively on the "tabernacle of David"—a tent David raised up where worship was offered up to the Lord continually. It was the place where the Ark of the Covenant, representing the glory of God, was placed until a more permanent temple was constructed during Solomon's reign.

Over the last few decades, an increasing number of believers have become involved in raising up houses of prayer, where worship and intercession are offered up to the Lord regularly, in some cases twenty-four hours per day and seven days per week. The vision for this movement is to create a resting place for the glory of God in the midst of His people. Those who teach about the tabernacle of David usually use Amos 9:11 as their key text:

"I will restore David's fallen shelter—I will repair its broken walls and restore its ruins—and will rebuild it as it used to be,

"so that they may possess the remnant of Edom and all the nations that bear my name," declares the Lord, who will do these things.

"The days are coming," declares the Lord, "when the reaper will be overtaken by the plowman and the planter by the one treading grapes. New wine will drip from the mountains and flow from all the hills,

"and I will bring my people Israel back from exile" (Amos 9:11-14 NIV).

First, this text clearly tells us that the specific model of worship that David used will be restored in the last days. This is why so many around the world have dedicated themselves to prophetic worship and intercession. However, the restoration of this model also comes with a series of remarkable promises. First, this text promises spiritual restoration, for the thing being "rebuilt as it used to be" is actually a people who desire to worship God and cry out to Him continually. Second, we see this people being restored **"so that they may possess the remnant . . . and all the nations that bear my name."** The end goal of the tabernacle of David is to restore the glory of God to a remnant of believers so that the remnant can "possess the nations" (also see Psalm 2). This point is made clearer in the next verse where we see a description of a harvest so great that there are not enough workers to bring it in.

Acts 15 clarifies that the apostles also used Amos 9:11 to lay out a clear vision of the harvest coming in from Gentile nations. However, when fully mature, the restoration of the tabernacle of David will be far more glorious than anything we see recorded in the Book of Acts.

I am thrilled to see the houses of prayer and worship being raised up around the world because these reveal the times we are living in. For just as David's tent was designed to host the Ark only until a more permanent temple could be raised up, our worship and intercession create a place for the presence of God to rest only until the literal New Jerusalem descends as a permanent resting place for God's glory. In this sense, our houses of prayer are a testimony that we are truly living at the end of the age. However, there is much more that God will add to this restoration as it reaches greater maturity.

The Thrones of the House of David

Just as we see the thrones of the twenty-four elders surrounding the Lord in Revelation 4, and the "thrones set in place" around the Ancient of Days in Daniel 7, we find that multiple thrones surrounded David in his ancient kingdom. The Psalmist declared:

I rejoiced with those who said to me, "Let us go to the house of the Lord."
Our feet are standing in your gates, Jerusalem.
Jerusalem is built like a city that is closely compacted together.
That is where the tribes go up—the tribes of the Lord—to praise the name of the Lord according to the statute given to Israel.
There stand the thrones for judgment, the thrones of the house of David (Psalm 122:1-5 NIV).

David had advisors specifically assigned to decree his commands and carry them out. These thrones faced David's throne, which was most likely elevated above them because he alone was the king. Just like David's advisors, we are called to rule and reign with Christ. We are called to behold His glory and hear what He is saying so that we can repeat His words from our own seat of spiritual authority.

From "Lukewarm" to "Sitting on the Throne"

This level of authority seems presumptuous and dangerous to the majority of believers because we have become satisfied with "mere salvation." We have not pressed in to the point that we can see, hear, and follow the living Christ. We are the generation that the living Christ rebukes for being "**lukewarm . . . wretched, pitiful, poor, blind, and naked**" (see Revelation 3:15, 18). However, in this same passage, Christ also gives us this invitation:

"I counsel you to buy from me gold refined in the fire, so you can become rich; and white clothes to wear, so you can cover your shameful nakedness; and salve to put on your eyes, so you can see.

"Those whom I love I rebuke and discipline. So be earnest and repent.

"Here I am! I stand at the door and knock. If anyone hears my voice and opens the door, I will come in and eat with that person, and they with me.

"To the one who is victorious, I will give the right to sit with me on my throne, just as I was victorious and sat down with my Father on his throne" (see Revelation 3:18-21 NIV).

Notice that Christ first invites us to become holy. He invites us to "buy gold," which speaks of a heart and mind completely purified and made radiant by His holy fire. He invites us to wear white clothes, which are acts of righteousness. And He invites us to put on eye salve so that we can have prophetic insight. He promises that when we do these things, we will have such sweet fellowship with Him that it will be like He is right in the room enjoying a meal with us. However, all of these things are simply foundations for us to rule and reign with Him.

Those who live holy lives and pursue deeper communion with Christ are given the right to sit with Him on His throne. This is nothing like Lucifer's aspiration, in which He sought to replace God and rebelled against His authority. Instead, Jesus explains that this is like when He sat down with the Father on His throne. Jesus sat down with the Father *after* He had fully yielded His will to Him on every matter. Likewise, the thing that opens the door for unprecedented spiritual authority in our lives is total submission to the Spirit of the living Christ.

Jesus is inviting us to sit with Him. Usually, when you sit on a chair, you are intending to park yourself there for quite a while. We often view spiritual authority as something we exercise only once in a while, at the height of a prayer meeting or in a moment when life's circumstances make us desperate. However, Christ is inviting us to park ourselves right in the middle of His will and not depart from it day or night. Those who truly learn to do this will bring great terror to the powers of darkness, even when they are saying nothing at all.

SMALL GROUP DISCUSSION QUESTIONS

Foundation Scripture One: Psalm 122

1. In the New Covenant, what is the "house of the Lord" (see I Peter 2:4-5)?

2. What does Jerusalem being "closely compacted together" reveal about the Lord's will for how we relate to others in the body of Christ? How do the "tribes going up" to worship in unity in Jerusalem relate to different streams, ministries, and denominations in the body of Christ?

3. Is our unity with each other related to the authority God will entrust to us? If so, how?

4. Why will cities and regions where the body of Christ is unified advance the kingdom of heaven more effectively (also see John 17:20-26)?

Foundation Scripture Two: Revelation 3:15-21

5. How do Christ's words in this passage speak directly to modern American culture?

6. How many different invitations from the Lord can you find in this passage? What instructions does Jesus give for accepting each unique invitation?

7. Which invitation are you drawn to the most? What does this reveal about your own calling and relationship with God?

8. What is the connection between relationship with God and authority? What is the connection between our relationship with others and authority?

The Coming "Christ Ministry"

If we have stopped building, it is because we have lost the blueprints. Over the past century, the body of Christ has seen dramatic advances. Each move of God has restored important biblical truths as God's people have sought Him in the midst of every move of the Spirit. Spiritual gifts have been restored to the church. The five-fold ministry has been restored. Great truths concerning spiritual authority, worship, intercession, and evangelism have been restored. Before we move on, it is good for us to look back and consider how far we have come in only the last few generations. The Lord has already restored the church in much greater ways than our great-grandparents could imagine.

Despite these advances, the church is still imperfect in its current state. Its love is lukewarm and its light is dim because its revelation of Christ is partial. Our thinking is often self-centered and shallow. I am reminded of Paul's reflection:

> For we know in part and we prophesy in part,
> but when perfection comes, the imperfect disappears.
> When I was a child, I thought like a child, I reasoned like a child. When I became a man, I put childish things behind me.

Now we see but a poor reflection as in a mirror; then we shall see face to face. Now I know in part; then I shall know fully, even as I am fully known.

And now these three remain: faith, hope, and love. But the greatest of these is love (I Corinthians 13:9-13 NIV).

You don't have to be a prophet to observe that our religious thinking is often petty and childish. However, pointing out the imperfections of the bride will never help her fulfill her destiny. In order to restore the bride to the full glory and perfection she is called to, we must reexamine the Father's blueprints for her.

Love and Longing

The Father's blueprints always entail more than mere instructions. When John was handed a scroll of revelation, he was told to eat it. It tasted like honey in his mouth but became bitter in his belly (see Revelation 10:9-10). This is a prophetic symbol describing any revelation we receive from the Lord. The initial experience of receiving revelation from God is thick, rich, and sweet like honey. We bask in the glory of what we encounter. However, the weight of what we have seen remains with us, as a holy irritant in the deepest seat of our thoughts and emotions until the revelation comes to pass. Every revelation from God comes with a corresponding longing in God's heart.

When we receive authentic revelation, we really receive a transference of love and longing from God's heart to ours. Even in the case of a warning, God shows us something out of the depths of His love for us. It is this love and longing of God that remains "bitter in our belly," causing us to travail in prayer and labor in ministry until it comes to pass.

Moving Beyond the Five-Fold Offices

In the past few decades, the focus has been on restoring

individual ministry offices, especially the offices of apostle and prophet. This is an incredibly important kind of restoration because the Scriptures tell us that apostles and prophets serve as the foundation of government for the body of Christ:

Now, therefore, you are no longer strangers and foreigners, but fellow citizens with the saints and members of the household of God,
having been built on the foundation of the apostles and prophets, Jesus Christ Himself being the chief cornerstone,
in whom the whole building, being fitted together, grows into a holy temple in the Lord,
in whom you also are being built together for a dwelling place of God in the Spirit (Ephesians 2:19-22).

Jesus Christ is the chief cornerstone because He is the "head" of the body of Christ. However, the way He rules over us in practical terms is by giving blueprints to His prophets and apostles so they can transmit a greater vision of the Father's house to all God's people.

Even though we rejoice in these advances, the raising up of apostles and prophets is not the end goal. The end goal is to build a "holy temple" of living stones where the Lord can dwell continually.

The Ephesians 4 Mandate

When giving a biblical defense for apostles and prophets, we most often quote from Ephesians:

And He Himself gave some to be apostles, some prophets, some evangelists, and some pastors and teachers,
for the equipping of the saints for the work of ministry (see Ephesians 4:11-12).

However, this chapter gives much more than a list of offices. The chapter begins with an explanation of how spiritual gifts and offices are dispersed:

> But to each one of us grace was given according to the measure of Christ's gift.
> Therefore He says: "When He ascended on high, He led captivity captive, and gave gifts to men" (Ephesians 4:7-8).

We each have been given a portion of Christ's ministry. Apostles have the architect portion. Prophets have the seer portion. Pastors have the shepherd portion. Teachers have the rabbi portion. Evangelists have the mercy portion. However, as long as we function as separate ministries, we will always be missing major aspects of who Christ is.

Now let's read the rest of the Ephesians 4 mandate:

> And He Himself gave some to be apostles, some prophets, some evangelists, and some pastors and teachers,
> for the equipping of the saints for the work of ministry, for the edifying of the body of Christ,
> till we all come to the unity of the faith and of the knowledge of the Son of God, to a perfect man, to the measure of the stature of the fullness of Christ;
> that we should no longer be children, tossed to and fro and carried about with every wind of doctrine, by the trickery of men, in the cunning craftiness of deceitful plotting,
> but, speaking the truth in love, may grow up in all things into Him who is the head—Christ—
> from whom the whole body, joined and knit together by what every joint supplies, according to the effective working by which every part does its share, causes growth of the body for the edifying of itself in love (Ephesians 4:11-16).

The Ephesians 4 mandate is circular when properly implemented. Christ distributes diverse gifts to all, the different portions of who He is. When we walk in our gifts and have unity, Christ is reassembled in our midst.

The end result of the Ephesians 4 mandate is that the body of Christ begins to function completely as Christ intended. This is what real maturity looks like.

When Jesus Prayed the Ephesians 4 Mandate

Although Paul was the most prolific author of the New Testament, it is good to go back to the words of Jesus, whom John G. Lake referred to as the "supreme court" of doctrine. In John 17, we find that Jesus' prayer to the Father lines up perfectly with Ephesians 4:

"My prayer is not for them alone. I pray also for those who will believe in me through their message,
"that all of them may be one, Father, just as you are in me and I am in you. May they also be in us so that the world may believe that you have sent me.
"I have given them the glory that you gave me, that they may be one as we are one—
"I in them and you in me—so that they may be brought to complete unity. Then the world will know that you sent me and have loved them even as you have loved me.
"Father, I want those you have given me to be with me where I am, and to see my glory, the glory you have given me because you loved me before the creation of the world.
"Righteous Father, though the world does not know you, I know you, and they know that you have sent me.
"I have made you known to them, and will continue to make you known in order that the love you have for me may be in them and that I myself may be in them" (John 17:20-26 NIV).

Notice that Jesus prayed for the same kind of unity and love that Ephesians 4 describes. He also further defines what maturity for His body on the earth looks like—abiding in love, unity, and the Father's glory all the time.

Jesus prayed that "**I myself may be in them**," and Paul defined maturity as "reaching the full measure of the stature of Christ" (see Ephesians 4:13). Ephesians 4 and John 17 both lead us to the same end goal—Christ completely revealed in us.

The Next Level for the Corporate Body of Christ

An angel of the harvest visited me while I was at the gym. He was filled with great joy as he showed me what was coming and gave me instructions for how to prepare for it. I set my weights down, sat on a bench, and began to see what he had to show me.

The first thing I saw was a fishing net with knuckle-sized knots in it. The angel said, "It is time to move from knuckle-sized knots to fist-sized knots." It took me about a week to process this, until I realized that these symbols referred to two different ways of understanding the five-fold ministry.

In the 1980s, many prophets and teachers used their hands to explain the five-fold ministry offices. The middle finger represented the evangelist because he goes the farthest in reaching people. The ring finger represented the pastor because he brings people to full commitment to the Lord and each other. The pinky finger represented the teacher because he can reach into every little place in the Word. The pointer finger spoke of the prophet's declaration. Finally, the thumb represented the apostle because he touches on the other offices as he builds the house of the Lord.

Knots are points of connection and speak of relationship in the body of Christ. The "knuckle-sized knots" are the kind of relationships we have had until now. Ministries and churches tend to gravitate to those of a similar calling or office. This has served a purpose for a season because prophetic ministries have learned from each other, teachers have worked together in bringing forth new restorations of truth, and so on. However, it is now time for an entirely new level of relationship.

The "fist-sized" knots speak of all the ministries working together in perfect synchronization—in the kind of unity and love envisioned in both John 17 and Ephesians 4. In order to properly steward the great harvest, we will need to be in relationship with *all* of the ministry offices.

The kind of unity that is coming is much more than politics and good intentions. The coming unity will be out of necessity. I am reminded of what happened when Peter was told to let out his nets for a large catch of fish:

When [Jesus] had finished speaking, he said to Simon, "Put out into deep water, and let down the nets for a catch."
Simon answered, "Master, we've worked hard all night and haven't caught anything. But because you say so, I will let down the nets."
When they had done so, they caught such a large number of fish that their nets began to break.
So they signaled their partners in the other boat to come and help them, and they came and filled both boats so full that they began to sink" (Luke 5:4-7 NIV).

When the fish are sparse, the fishermen are very territorial. They fight over who gets the fish and stake out their designated fishing spots. When the fish are plentiful, as in this passage, the fishermen must partner together to bring in the harvest or else they will sink from the weight of it. This is the new reality we are about to step into as the next move of God unfolds.

The territorialism that has marked churches and ministries in the last few decades will quickly fade as the Lord releases a harvest of souls weightier than we have imagined. In order to reach, disciple, and train each new believer, we will need every church, ministry and individual believer positioned where they belong in the body of Christ.

For those who have spent decades in the body of Christ, this kind of unity may seem unattainable and little more than blind optimism. However, we have yet to see the other aspects of what Jesus prayed—a deeper revelation of Christ's glory and a greater revelation of the Father. In order to bring about this new level of unity and form these fist-sized knots, the Lord is first going to release a revelation of His glory that completely shatters our old religious mindsets and turns us back to our first love. He is going to restore our individual relationships with the Father so magnificently that when we come together, we will be brothers and sisters because we have already been made legitimate sons and daughters.

The Next Level for Individual Ministries

Once the glory returns, sonship will return (see Romans 8). Once sonship returns, the offices will change dramatically in how they function. The different ministries will be more powerful than anyone could have prophesied, but they will be less noticeable because someone else will be taking all of the attention—the Lord Jesus Christ.

Healing revivalists, such as Kathryn Kuhlman and William Branham, have described moments when "Jesus stepped into them." In some cases, they watched great miracles take place as if they were outside observers. This is because "Jesus the Healer" stepped into them. This is the highest expression of the Christ ministry. However, this kind of Christ ministry is not reserved only for healing ministries or evangelists. What will happen

> *Imagine what would happen if everyone in the body was made so holy that they actually heard Christ clearly and obeyed all the time.*

when intercessors allow Christ the High Priest to pray through them? What will happen when prophets allow Christ to reveal hidden mysteries through them? What will happen when apostles allow Christ the Architect and Builder to design through them? As God releases greater dimensions of holiness, we must seek closer connection with Christ in every gift and ministry.

This is an inheritance that is available to every one in the body of Christ, and it does not require a platform to work. If you have the gift of hospitality or helps, you can invite Jesus to cook and clean through you. As a prophetic writer, I feel closest to the Lord when I am writing. However, I am also aware of Christ's ministry when I'm washing dishes or working in the garden. This is the deeper communion with Jesus we all have the opportunity to enjoy in this life.

Imagine what would happen if everyone in the body was made so holy that they actually heard Christ clearly and obeyed all the time. Leaders would already be in agreement before they began speaking. Individual believers would be in the right place, at the right time, all the time. A great cloud of glory would descend upon this fully-submitted body of Christ until Jesus could step into this house of living stones and move through it continually. This, my friends, is the next level—and in some places, we are almost there.

Small Group Discussion Questions

Foundation Scripture One: Ephesians 4:1-16

1. Who is the ultimate source of every ministry gift and office? Why was it important for Christ to ascend to the right hand of the Father?

2. What is the ultimate purpose of the five ministry offices in this passage (see verses 12-13)?

3. Can any of the five-fold ministry offices fulfill its calling in isolation from the others? Why or why not?

4. Why will it be increasingly important to develop strong spiritual unity as the end-times harvest unfolds?

5. Which ministry office are you most drawn to? Why?

6. What steps can we take as a group to prepare for the great harvest of souls about to flood into the kingdom?

Foundation Scripture Two: John 17:20-26

7. Who was Jesus praying for in this passage? Does it include us?

8. What did He pray concerning our relationships with each other?

9. What did He pray about our relationship with the Father?

10. What did He pray concerning our outreach to others?

11. What can we do as a group to fulfill Christ's intercession in this passage?

The Ancient Gatekeepers 8

Lift up your heads, you gates; be lifted up, you ancient doors, that the King of glory may come in. Who is this King of glory? The Lord strong and mighty, the Lord mighty in battle.

Lift up your heads, you gates; lift them up, you ancient doors, that the King of glory may come in.

Who is he, this King of glory? The Lord Almighty— he is the King of glory (Psalm 24:7-10 NIV).

There is a strange dichotomy in this Scripture. One would expect every head to be bowed low when the "King of glory" shows up. Instead, the "heads of the gates" are commanded to be "lifted up." One interpretation is that the gates represent key "gate-keeper" ministries in the body of Christ.

When the glory of God returns to the body of Christ, it does not mean that every ministry will cease to exist—it means that every ministry will be glorified to fulfill its true purpose. Key leaders will be lifted up to a greater extent so they may fulfill their role in preparing the way of the Lord.

The 212 Gatekeepers

I also believe that these "gates" refer to specific gatekeepers, which we find a prophetic template for in the Old Testament. The Scriptures describe an ancient line of gatekeepers who specifically held the keys to the temple treasuries. These gatekeepers were raised up by King David and Samuel the prophet:

> Altogether, those chosen to be gatekeepers at the thresholds numbered 212. They were registered by genealogy in their villages. The gatekeepers had been assigned to their positions of trust by David and Samuel the seer.
> They and their descendants were in charge of guarding the gates of the house of the Lord—the house called the tent of meeting.
> The gatekeepers were on the four sides: east, west, north and south.
> Their fellow Levites in their villages had to come from time to time and share their duties for seven-day periods.
> But the four principal gatekeepers, who were Levites, were entrusted with the responsibility for the rooms and treasuries in the house of God.
> They would spend the night stationed around the house of God, because they had to guard it; and they had charge of the key for opening it each morning.
> Some of them were in charge of the articles used in the temple service; they counted them when they were brought in and when they were taken out.
> Others were assigned to take care of the furnishings and all the other articles of the sanctuary, as well as the special flour and wine, and the olive oil, incense and spices.
> But some of the priests took care of mixing the spices.
> A Levite named Mattithiah, the firstborn son of Shallum the Korahite, was entrusted with the responsibility for baking the offering bread.
> Some of the Kohathites, their fellow Levites, were in charge

> *The gatekeepers of the temple had apostolic and prophetic authority because they were under apostolic and prophetic authority.*

of preparing for every Sabbath the bread set out on the table.

Those who were musicians, heads of Levite families, stayed in the rooms of the temple and were exempt from other duties because they were responsible for the work day and night (I Chronicles 9:22-33 NIV).

There are several important patterns in this text from which we can glean insight into the "gatekeepers" the Lord is raising up.

1. The gatekeepers were guards.

Specific "gatekeepers" were set in place to guard the tabernacle day and night. They were both protectors and overseers.

2. The gatekeepers had apostolic and prophetic authority because they were under apostolic and prophetic authority.

These gatekeepers were raised up by King David, who represents apostolic authority, and Samuel the seer, who represents prophetic authority. When the earth swallowed up Korah and his followers in Numbers 16, it demonstrated what happens when a priestly gatekeeper actively opposes someone in spiritual authority. Korah and his men were also assigned to be gatekeepers of the temple, but they opposed Moses and Aaron's authority instead of respecting them (see Numbers 16).

The Bible warns us of false apostles and false prophets. However, we also see in the Word a blueprint for the government of God that is built on the foundation of the apostles and the prophets. In this sense, they function as ministries that support and protect everything that God is doing in the earth.

3. The gatekeepers had access to all that was holy and were involved in bringing it into active service.

These gatekeepers were in charge of taking out the articles used in the temple service and mixing the unique incenses and spices used in service to the Lord. The gatekeepers that the Lord is now raising up will bring new revelation of ancient mysteries into the houses of prayer, empowering the saints to reach new levels of worship, intercession, and prophetic declaration.

As the tabernacle of David reaches the next stage, we will see the Lord raising up people anointed to bring new fragrances and expressions of the kingdom back into His house. Some will even unlock the door to the Lord's vast treasury rooms—many are ancient mysteries lost in time or manifestations of the glory beyond what we dreamed was possible. In some places, it will literally look and feel like heaven landed on earth. However, this is nothing more than the gatekeepers using the key of David to open heaven's gates and close the gates of hell.

The Reigning Councils and the Glory

I share these things because the blueprint that the Father has shown me is one in which He establishes "reigning councils" in different regions overseen by prophetic gatekeepers who abide in the fellowship and counsel of the living Christ all the time. When they meet together in holy council, it is as if they are seated in thrones of authority around Him. Whatever they declare in these councils will be permanently established as a matter of law. If they close a gate of hell, it remains closed. If they bind something, it remains bound. If they open the gates to heaven over a region, it remains open until the Lord accomplishes everything that He desires to accomplish there. The angels gather around them to find their next assignments and instructions. This is nothing less than the Lord's mountain of governance being raised up above every other mountain.

The tabernacle of David is already raised up and prepared for the glory to come back. These reigning councils will be the priests whose shoulders will carry the Ark. These are the holy ones being raised up—even from among the most bound and desperate people suffering in the most miserable of spiritual conditions. He is going to give them gold refined in the fire, purifying their hearts and minds. He is going to clothe them in complete righteousness. He is going to come in and feast with them every day. But last, He is going to give them the right to sit on thrones of authority around Him, so that everything in their sphere of influence on earth will be impacted by the glory that they carry.

The Bible speaks clearly and repeatedly concerning "elders at the gate." We have already seen the pattern of the elders in heaven. Now it is time to raise up elders who can open and close spiritual gates on the earth with decisive prophetic authority. Over the last few decades, we have focused on building the structure that will house the glory—the tabernacle of David. However, the Ark that is coming back is actually a *throne for the glory*. The level of presence, power, and authority that the Spirit of Holiness brings will carry the same resurrection power that raised Jesus from the dead. We will know these elders because they will sitting and declaring what the living Christ is declaring at a time when no one else is able to stand from the penetrating glory of God in our midst.

These will be the holy ones who "lift up their heads" so that **"the King of glory may come in"** (see Psalm 24:7). Only then will the Lord will reveal Himself as **"mighty in battle"** (see Psalm 24:8). When we build a place for Him to rest in the fullness of

His glory in a region, nothing can stand in His way.

The ultimate purpose of these reigning councils will be to serve as gatekeepers fully dedicated to ensuring that Christ receives the reward of His sufferings in the earth. This model is completely at odds with our religious tradition. This is because we consider humble service to only include changing lightbulbs and washing toilets. The reality is that many of the holy ones will rule and reign with Him at the same time that they are changing lightbulbs and washing toilets. The Christ that we serve was as comfortable washing feet as He is now sitting on His throne in matchless glory. The holy people will be completely comfortable and at peace, whether they are serving others out of selfless love or bringing back the glory with unprecedented spiritual authority—their eyes will be fixed on the eternal realm, not the things of this world.

I have simply painted a portrait of what it will look like when we take Christ's words at face value:

"Truly I tell you, whatever you bind on earth will be bound in heaven, and whatever you loose on earth will be loosed in heaven.
"Again, truly I tell you that if two of you on earth agree about anything they ask for, it will be done for them by my Father in heaven.
"For where two or three gather in my name, there am I with them" (Matthew 18:18-20).

It is time to become holy people and live according to the pattern that Christ gave us—where only two or three people gathered together can literally close the gates to hell or open the gates to heaven.

SMALL GROUP DISCUSSION QUESTIONS

Foundation Scripture One: Psalm 24

1. How will the body of Christ change when the "King of Glory" reveals Himself more fully to us?

2. What can we do individually to make room for the King of Glory to be revealed in our personal lives, our families, or our spheres of influence?

3. What can we do as the body of Christ to make room for the King of Glory to inhabit our churches and ministries, our city, and our region?

Foundation Scripture Two: Matthew 18:18-20

4. Are there any doors of sin, compromise, or demonic influence in your life that you need help closing?

5. Provide a time for repentance and prayers of agreement to close these "doors."

6. What kind of relationship with God to your desire to have? What aspects of your calling to you want to focus on fulfilling in the next year?

7. Provide a time for invoking God's presence and prayers of agreement to open new doors to the Holy Spirit and to angelic ministry in each person's life.

Walking With the Holy One

Finding the Highway of Holiness 9

Many believers are conditioned to look for the next mountaintop experience, such as a moment at a revival meeting, an amazing miracle, or an extremely accurate prophetic word. After this brief moment of encounter, we descend back into our mundane and ordinary lives. However, this descent is a choice.

God will allow you to live a mundane and ordinary life with the occasional mountaintop experience if that is all you desire. However, I have written this book for those who hunger for much more than this. This spiritual hunger is the surest sign that you are called to a much higher spiritual position—one where you remain close to the Lord all the time. It is good to make a pilgrimage to the mountain. However, the Lord wants to use these experiences to teach us to abide in Him all the time.

The Highway and the High Call

Paul described the higher calling that he reached for in this way:

> Brethren, I do not count myself to have apprehended: but this one thing I do, forgetting those things which are behind,

and reaching forth unto those things which are before,

I press toward the mark for the prize of the high calling of God in Christ Jesus (Philippians 3:13-14).

When Paul wrote this, he had already encountered the living Christ and had a clear revelation of heaven. He had planted hundreds of churches, healed the sick, performed great signs and wonders, and preached the Gospel throughout much of the civilized world. His writings show that he had already attained a depth of revelation about God. So what was Paul reaching for here?

First, Paul was looking to remain in step with the Spirit to be part of the next move of God. He was "**reaching forth unto those things which are before.**" He chose to forget what he had accomplished in the past in order to focus on what God wanted to do next. He was not content to rest on his laurels because he knew there were even greater things to accomplish in the future.

It is good to make a pilgrimage to the mountain. However, the Lord wants to use our mountain top experiences to teach us to abide in Him all the time.

That was not all Paul reached for. His greatest desire was to find "**the prize of the high calling of God.**" There are two ways to interpret this phrase. First, the "**prize of the high calling**" may simply refer to Paul's reward in heaven. Perhaps he wanted to continue serving God to receive a greater reward in heaven. This is how most Christians interpret this text. However, I believe that the "**high calling of God**" is itself a prize worth reaching for. For once we have truly learned to abide in God, once we have learned to gaze into His penetrating light, life, and love all the time, we lay hold of an eternal communion that will place its grip on every part of our nature and never let go.

The Highway of Holiness

The best description I've found for the "high calling of God" is in Isaiah 35. Isaiah describes the "Highway of Holiness" in great detail, including how to get on it, how to stay on it, and where it will lead you. I consider the "high calling" and the "way of holiness" to describe the same thing—a way to walk with God and abide in His Holiness continually. Isaiah declared:

And a highway will be there; it will be called the Way of Holiness. The unclean will not journey on it; it will be for those who walk in that Way; wicked fools will not go about on it.
No lion will be there, nor will any ferocious beast get up on it; they will not be found there. But only the redeemed will walk there,
and the ransomed of the Lord will return. They will enter Zion with singing; everlasting joy will crown their heads. Gladness and joy will overtake them, and sorrow and sighing will flee away (Isaiah 35:8-10 NIV).

The Highway of Holiness is a walk with God positioned above every force of darkness. No lion, ferocious beast, or wicked fool can come near it. This does not mean we will not face trials, persecution, or turmoil in this life. It means that we will abide in the perfect peace, presence, and power of God even in hard times.

No demon of hell or force of darkness can affect the hearts and minds of those who walk on this highway because they walk continually in a spiritual position established far above these powers. The Bible makes it clear that we are "seated with Christ in heavenly places" (see Ephesians 2:6), but we are often content to take that position only once in a while.

This is not a walk where we remain frozen in a perfect state, like a beatified saint on display. This walk leads us uphill, through hidden and dark places and against great odds. The journey is designed to be difficult so that only those truly desiring to be closer to the Lord will continue on it. The path is designed to be narrow, traveling through perilous places to expose and remove the worst parts of our nature. This Highway of Holiness will ultimately transform us to reflect the glorious image of Christ. This journey will cause us to shed the carnal wood, hay, and stubble in our lives and bring forth the gold, silver, and costly stones of eternal value. It will cause us to reject the darkness as one rejects a virus, and open us up to the exceeding and penetrating light of the living Christ, the ultimate antidote to all that ails us.

The goal of the next few chapters is to lay out a few "on-ramps" to this Highway of Holiness. Despite the perils, the Highway of Holiness is a path of ascent. As we abide in the Spirit of Holiness, we draw closer to greater revelation of who He is and what He is doing. Our desires become purified until we are more driven by the Lord's desire than by our own.

Moving to Maturity

Spiritual gifts are important for every believer to understand and operate in. The gifts are like construction tools—it is difficult to build anything of spiritual significance without them. The gifts may also function as weapons, allowing us to intercede effectively, discern the enemy's plans, and dismantle them. Above all, the gifts allow us to draw near to God for ourselves. However, even the gifts of the Spirit are a mere overflow of the deeper deposit the Father has placed in us.

I saw this more clearly during a recent time of prayer. As I was strumming my guitar, an overwhelming peace flooded the room. It felt like a warm blanket with a real weight that made it gloriously difficult to move. I soon fell into a deep slumber, with my guitar still in my hands.

I was immediately taken to a white table with different firearms laid out for inspection. The weapons were clean, well-oiled, and used regularly. I smiled because I felt God's pleasure with these weapons. As I examined them, I thought, *"nothing will be impossible for us as long as we keep these weapons clean and keep using them."* As I admired the weapons, I realized that there was a basement under me that I was unaware of. In this basement, there was an expanding cloud of fire that looked like an atom bomb exploding in slow motion. The light and glory of heaven was in the middle of this cloud. It was infinitely more powerful—and more dangerous—than any of the weapons on the table. When I saw this expanding fire, I knew that it would continue growing until everything in its path was made holy and aligned with heaven.

It is good for us to steward our spiritual gifts well. We are meant to use our gifts frequently and effectively, just like a soldier's clean and well-oiled weapons. Prophetic prayers or tongues can be powerful and effective weapons against the forces of darkness. The weapons are effective in their purpose. However, the cloud of fire has a much greater purpose, and consequently, a much greater power. Nothing could stand in its way.

When the gifts of the Spirit operate in our lives, it is obvious to ourselves and everyone around us. However, the deeper work of the Spirit of Holiness begins in our "basement," or our base nature. This expanding cloud of fire in the basement speaks of the Spirit of Holiness working inside of us, often beyond our awareness or comprehension. If we allow the Spirit of Holiness to inhabit our deepest desires, then His fire and glory will begin to consume everything else in our lives. If we continually invoke His presence and yield to Him when He comes, then we allow this "fire in the basement" to completely regenerate our nature.

As a result, the fire of holiness begins to light our whole house on fire.

Beyond the Gifts of the Spirit

In the 1980s and 1990s, most teachers emphasized the gifts of the Spirit because the body needed it at the time. However, my purpose is to reclaim an aspect of the Holy Spirit needed in the next move of God: His desire is to make us holy.

The gifts of the Spirit cannot be the highest or most important expression of the Spirit that we receive. Jesus tells us:

"Not everyone who says to me, 'Lord, Lord,' will enter the kingdom of heaven, but only the one who does the will of my Father who is in heaven.
"Many will say to me on that day, 'Lord, Lord, did we not prophesy in your name and in your name drive out demons and in your name perform many miracles?'
"Then I will tell them plainly, 'I never knew you. Away from me, you evildoers!'" (Matthew 7:21-23 NIV)

Jesus refers to the gifts of the Spirit operating in great power here—people were prophesying, driving out demons, and performing miracles. The problem is that He never knew them. They were operating in the gifts, but they never pressed in to become fully acquainted with the living Christ who walks among the golden candlesticks. This is why Jesus says, **"I never knew you"** in past tense. He is basically saying, "You operated in great gifts of the Spirit, but you never sought to really know Me."

They also did not seek deeper relationship with the Father, for they did not do the Father's will. In other words, they had a shallow version of spirituality. They viewed the gifts of the Spirit as their highest accomplishment while neglecting the higher pursuit of intimate friendship with the Father and Son. Sadly, many believers are waiting until Christ returns—or until they die—to become acquainted with the Father and the Son. These are the kind of believers that Christ will command to "depart from Him" because He "never knew them."

The Highest Expression of the Spirit

Love is the highest expression of the Spirit that we can receive. This is why Paul introduced the "love chapter" in I Corinthians 13 by saying: **"And now I will show you the most excellent way."** (see I Corinthians 12:31 NIV)

In context, this verse follows immediately after chapter 12 where Paul lists the gifts of the Spirit, explains them, and gives specific instructions for how they should function. These things were important to share, but they were not the "most excellent" thing he shared.

Paul begins his description of love by contrasting it with a powerful demonstration of spiritual gifts:

If I speak in the tongues of men or of angels, but do not have love, I am only a resounding gong or a clanging cymbal.
If I have the gift of prophecy and can fathom all mysteries and all knowledge, and if I have a faith that can move mountains, but do not have love, I am nothing.
If I give all I possess to the poor and give over my body to hardship that I may boast, but do not have love, I gain nothing (I Corinthians 13:1-3 NIV).

Paul goes on to describe all the dimensions of love, which are similar to the fruit of the Spirit.

Love is patient, love is kind. It does not envy, it does not boast, it is not proud.
It does not dishonor others, it is not self-seeking, it is

not easily angered, it keeps no record of wrongs.

Love does not delight in evil but rejoices with the truth.

It always protects, always trusts, always hopes, always perseveres.

Love never fails (see I Corinthians 13:4-8 NIV).

It is easy to see why someone prophesying or working miracles is in trouble if they are not living by this description. Unfortunately, this has been the case in many fellowships, where believers will prophesy or speak in tongues one minute and begin gossiping or criticizing others in the next. This list seems like a tall order, but these are side effects of something much deeper as the Spirit of Holiness works to reveal love to our base nature. However, even this great magnitude of love, this highest expression of the Spirit, is a mere side effect of something even deeper.

The Fire in Paul's Basement

In the last section of the chapter, we find the fire that was in Paul's basement:

For we know in part and we prophesy in part, but when perfection comes, the imperfect disappears.

When I was a child, I talked like a child, I thought like a child, I reasoned like a child. When I became a man, I put childish things behind me.

Now, we see but a poor reflection as in a mirror; then we shall see face to face. Now I know in part; then I show know fully, even as I am fully known.

Now, these three remain: faith, hope, and love. But the greatest of these is love.

Follow the way of love and eagerly desire spiritual gifts, especially the gift of prophecy. (I Corinthians 13:9-14:1).

The fire in Paul's "basement" was a burning desire to know Christ more intimately. He longed to "see Him face to face" and be "fully known" by Him. This burning desire allowed him to encounter the depths of Christ's love, opening the door to the wisdom and revelation we see in his epistles. Unless we begin to live by this same kind of desire, we will remain shallow and childish. However, if we kindle the fires of desire in our deepest longings, we will begin to find a deeper level of intimacy and freedom in Christ that will gradually expand to purify our whole house.

Making "Christ in Us" a Living Reality

The mystery that has been kept hidden for ages and generations, but is now disclosed to the Lord's people.
To them God has chosen to make known among the Gentiles the glorious riches of this mystery, which is Christ in you, the hope of glory (Colossians 1:26-27 NIV).

Most believers are taught that Christ is "in" them. However, our response to this is often an intellectual acknowledgement that it is true. We acknowledge that the seed is there, but we do not water it so that it will grow. If "Christ in us" was merely an intellectual premise, then it would not entail "glorious riches" and "hidden mysteries." These treasures can only be unveiled when we activate and engage the seed God planted in us when we gave our lives to Him.

The rising holy ones will overcome the world because they will have a spiritual understanding of the living Christ who abides in them. They will see that His seed is living, active, and full of glory. Their longing for Him will germinate the seed so that it begins to grow in them. As a result, they will experience the kind of love Paul encountered and access levels of gifting beyond anything seen before. The seed will grow in size and intensity until His Presence transforms everything they think, say, or do. They will encounter the glory they hope for and access the hidden treasures of revelation that other generations longed to discover.

Putting the Lamp on Its Stand

"No one, when he has lit a lamp, puts it in a secret place or under a basket, but on a lampstand, that those who come in may see the light" (Luke 11:33 NIV).

Jesus told us that we should not keep our lamp hidden or hide it under a basket. We usually apply this Scripture to evangelism and assume it means that we should not hide our light from others. This is a good principle to live by, but it is not what Jesus was talking about. In the next verse, He gives this interpretation:

"The lamp of the body is the eye. Therefore, when your eye is good, your whole body also is full of light. But when your eye is bad, your body also is full of darkness" (Luke 11:34 NIV).

The way we "hide our light under a basket" is by allowing other things to become more important than Christ in us. The troubles of life, with all of its stresses and anxieties, are like a basket the enemy weaves to distract us from becoming who we are called to be. When we become sidetracked by these distractions, we become apathetic in our faith—the light remains a flicker and the seed remains dormant. For others, the basket that hides the light of Christ in them is the intellectual mindset of traditional Western Christianity. This basket is made of strong cords of unbelief, rationalism, and skepticism.

A "stand" is a place of honor, like a pedestal. The way that we allow the light of "Christ in us" to grow is by giving Him more attention than anything else in our lives. When we keep our eyes fixed on Him, then our eyes become "good" because the One we are looking at is good.

SMALL GROUP DISCUSSION QUESTIONS

Foundation Scripture One: Philippians 3:14

1. What does the "high calling of God" look like for you?

2. Are there things in your past you need to "forget" in order to fulfill your high calling? (Is there anything holding you back?)

3. What is the "holy fire in your basement?" Describe your deepest spiritual longings and desires.

4. What can you do each day to nurture the fire God has already placed in you?

Foundation Scripture Two: I Corinthians 12:31-14:1
Note: This passage includes one verse preceding and one verse following I Corinthians 13.

5. Taken in context, does I Corinthians 13 de-emphasize the importance of spiritual gifts? If not, then what is the purpose of this passage?

6. What "way" must we follow to lay hold of the "greater gifts" (see I Corinthians 14:1)?

7. How is Paul's description of love in I Corinthians 13 similar to the list of fruits of the Spirit in Galatians 5:22-23? How is it different?

8. What kind of revelation is Paul referring to when he proclaims, "When perfection comes, the imperfect disappears…?" (verse 10)

The Redemption of Desire   10

The work of the cross began in the garden of Gethsemane, where Jesus prayed so intensely that His sweat mingled with drops of blood. It is good for us to emphasize the salvation and healing the cross offers, which remain foundations for all that follows. However, Gethsemane revealed the deeper implications of Christ's redemption, which include a completely regenerated heart, mind, and spirit. Here in the garden, we find the keys for truly overcoming the world and walking with the Father each day as Jesus did. Let us look closer at what happened there. The Apostle Luke explains:

> An angel from heaven appeared to Him and strengthened Him.
> And being in agony He was praying very fervently; and His sweat became like drops of blood, falling down upon the ground (Luke 22:43-44 NAS).

In order to understand what happened here, we must first realize that everything Christ suffered symbolized a specific aspect of His atonement. For example, His death stripped the power of death from our lives. The thirty-nine lashes He suffered on His back purchased our healing from the thirty-nine classifications of disease. The blood-soaked scarlet robe placed on Him signifies that He took the sins of the world upon Himself. The crown of thorns on His head represented the removal of the original curse placed on all of creation. Christ's internal suffering in the garden of Gethsemane was just as significant as the external aspects of His atonement we usually focus on.

Where Christ Yielded His Will

Christ yielded His will completely to the Father in the garden of Gethsemane. The Apostle Matthew explains:

Then Jesus came with them to a place called Gethsemane, and said to the disciples, "Sit here while I go and pray over there."
And He took with Him Peter and the two sons of Zebedee, and He began to be sorrowful and deeply distressed.
Then He said to them, "My soul is exceedingly sorrowful, even to death. Stay here and watch with Me."
He went a little farther and fell on His face, and prayed, saying, "O My Father, if it is possible, let this cup pass from Me; nevertheless, not as I will, but as You will" (Matthew 26:36-39).

This moment involved more than Christ simply yielding His own will—He had already lived His entire life in perfect submission to the Father. His anguish increased to the point where he "sweated drops of blood" in the moment when He willingly took upon Himself the heavy weight of all our sin, our bondages, and the curse of the Fall.

Luke tells us that **"an angel from heaven appeared to Christ and strengthen Him"** (see Luke 22:43) just before His internal suffering reached the point of shedding blood. This angel was sent by the Father, who wanted to give Christ one last glimpse of the holy people He was redeeming at the very moment that His lips touched the cup of our suffering for the first time—when

He shed the first drops of blood mingled with sweat. I believe this angelic herald showed Christ one last glimpse of the New Jerusalem, for the glory of this city has the power to strengthen us to endure all manner of suffering in its pursuit. For Christ, the intoxicating beauty of His bride was the only thing worth dying for. Ultimately, Gethsemane involved Christ choosing to lose Himself so fully in His desire for us that He was willing to suffer and die. This is why John defines love through Christ's sacrifice:

This is how we know what love is: Jesus Christ laid down His life for us (see I John 3:16).

Love is rooted in pure and holy desire for another. The kind of spiritual love we can experience is the power of Christ's desire for us. It is like the romantic love of a young man for his bride. It is impossible to explore Christ's love without the force of His desire impacting and transforming our own desires. However, in order to fully understand the mystery of what happened at Gethsemane, we have to go back to the beginning.

Man's Sovereignty and Original Sin

Mankind was given free will at creation. Many theologians refer to this concept as the "sovereignty of man" because we were created with the freedom to choose our destiny. The Father placed two trees in the garden because He was not looking for robots—He wanted mankind to choose Him over everything else. From the beginning, He wanted mankind to love Him out of desire, not compulsion.

We do not know how many years Adam and Eve enjoyed sweet communion with God before they chose to disobey Him. However, we know that they became so familiar with Him that they even recognized the sound of His approach (see Genesis 3:8).

We usually consider the "original sin" to be the first bite Eve took from the fruit of the tree of the knowledge of good and evil. However, Eve's will became corrupted even before she took the bite. The original sin did not begin with the first bite—it began when Eve's desires turned to something else.

> *The original sin did not begin with the first bite—it began when Eve's desires turned to something else.*

The Bible tells us that the serpent was **"more crafty"** (see Genesis 3:1) than any other creature. This is not a fable with talking animals. The serpent was the real and tangible form the fallen angel Lucifer took to deceive her. In Hebrew, the word for serpent is *nachash*, which comes from the same root word as "shining."[3] Lucifer did not appear as the kind of slimy, slithering snake that repulses us today. He appeared as a beautiful and colorful winged serpent shining with otherworldly light, a creature that God commanded would no longer exist in its former state after the Fall.

His deception was specifically designed to corrupt Eve's desires by enticing her with a lesser form of beauty, beginning with his own deceptively beautiful appearance. Lucifer succeeded with this kind of enticement, which is why Eve **"saw that the fruit of the tree was good for food and pleasing to the eye, and also desirable for gaining wisdom"** (see Genesis 3:6). In other words, the original sin began with the perversion of desire and beauty before Adam and Eve even took their first bite.

Understanding "Free Will"

We have all been given "free will" by God. Our will is our own sovereign internal decider that may be used for good or evil.

3 Dr. Ray Stedman, "The Enticement of Evil," www.RayStedman.org.

We exert our free will every time we make a decision. However, our free will does not exist in a vacuum. Our will is the expression of our deepest thoughts, emotions, longings, and desires. The thousands of decisions that we make every day flow out of our core desires. The introduction of sin and death into the world, and the corruption of the heart of man, began with a corruption of desire.

If the Fall of man began with the corruption of desire, then it makes sense that the atoning work of Christ would begin with the redemption of desire. When Christ took our sins upon Himself, He experienced the full weight of our unwholesome desires. This is why the Scriptures clearly tell us:

Because He himself suffered when he was tempted, he is able to help those who are being tempted (Hebrews 2:18 NIV).

For we do not have a high priest who is unable to empathize with our weaknesses, but we have one who has been tempted in every way, just as we are—yet he did not sin (Hebrews 4:15 NIV).

Notice that these texts clearly tell us that Christ was tempted in every way. In Gethsemane, Christ willingly took upon Himself all of the unwholesome desires of mankind, accumulated through the ages. The weight of this baggage was enough to make Him "sorrowful to the point of death." This is why He desired companionship just to make it through the night. However, in the end, His desire to please the Father and remain in perfect unity with Him was greater than the accumulated unwholesome desires of human history. In this sense, the garden of Gethsemane involved a monumental transaction. The Lord Jesus Christ exchanged our unwholesome desires for the one simple and pure desire to please the Father.

The atoning work of Christ offers more than forgiveness of sin: His atonement offers us complete and total deliverance from sin's entanglement. As a result, we can be completely delivered from our own carnality in this life. We can choose to banish unwholesome desires from our lives and replace them with a burning hunger and thirst to know God more.

Once our desire for God becomes stronger than everything else, there is no going back. This redemption of our desires is like a golden root planted in our hearts. Eventually, this golden root of holy desire will displace every *unholy* thing in our hearts and minds.

Yielding Our Will Through Holy Desire

Gethsemane was not a religious performance—it was an example of how choosing the right thing to desire frees us to yield our will to the Father. Consider what David wrote:

> **Sacrifice and offering you did not desire—but my ears you have opened—burnt offerings and sin offerings you did not require.**
> **Then I said, "Here I am, I have come—it is written about me in the scroll.**
> **"I desire to do your will, my God; your law is within my heart"** (Psalm 40:6-8 NIV).

David clarifies that sacrifice for religion's sake is not desirable to God. Prayer, fasting, or other spiritual disciplines have no value if they become mere religious obligations (see Isaiah 58). The Father only values the kind of sacrifice that flows from burning desire.

The Bible tells us that David was "a man after God's own heart." However, he developed this kind of godliness by yielding his desires to the Father and seeking His will on every matter. This is why we read that David **"inquired of the Lord"** before almost everything he did (see I Samuel 23:4; II Samuel 2:1, 5:19-23, and I Chronicles 14:10-14). If we want to be like David, then we must first cultivate the desire to yield to God's will in every matter.

The reason it is often difficult to do the Father's will instead of our own is because we love other things much more than we love Him. As long as we continue to "chase after other lovers" (see Hosea 2:7), we probably will not hear from Him clearly—if at all.

The idea of having a "balanced" life, in which God is just a box to be checked on Sunday morning, is an affront to the living God of the Bible. The concept of having "religious" and "secular" categories in our life is deeply embedded in our Western mindsets, but this concept is not found anywhere in the Bible. Many of today's churches simply repackage "self-help" teaching to fill the pews. We are taught principles that will make us more balanced, healthy, wealthy, and happy. The problem is that most of these teachings hinder us from pursuing the kingdom of God—they turn our desires to everything but our true love. As a result, we have beautiful homes, great relationships, lots of money, and a vast and aching hole in our lives where God belongs.

The truth is that we cannot really know God or serve Him unless we make Him the primary object of our affections all the time. This is why Jesus told us that the greatest commandment is:

"Love the Lord your God with all your heart and with all your soul and with all your mind and with all your strength" (Mark 12:30).

Notice that Jesus taught us to love the Father with our whole being—with *all* of our heart, with *all* of our soul, and with *all* of our mind (some translations say with *all* of our strength). This means that our pursuit of God has the potential to encompass all of our emotions, the deepest longings and travails of our soul, our thought-life, and our daily activities. When we dedicate these aspects of ourselves to God, then He comes to inhabit them. We can give our desires to God and let Him mold them like clay. We can allow Him to free us from desire for unwholesome things—or even "good" distractions—so that we may be filled with desire for more revelation of His beauty and glory. We can surrender our thought-life to Him and ask Him to inhabit and direct our thoughts towards Him. We can reorganize our lives in a way that places a higher priority on Him than on anything else.

Fasting to Break Unwholesome Desires

Fasting breaks the power of desire for whatever we happen to be fasting for. If we fast food or sleep so that we can pray, then we consciously exert our free will to take back our desires and turn them to God. However, our fasting does not need to be limited to food or sleep. One of the most difficult fasts that I went on happened when the Father asked me to fast Internet coverage of politics for a few months. I had developed such a love for tracking politics that it became an addiction that captivated my desire. After a few months of setting this pursuit aside, I found that the addictive desire to know what was going on in politics was overshadowed by a greater desire to know what was going on in the Father's heart. The Father began to show me what *He* thought about our political situation until my strongest views began to change. There is nothing wrong with food, sleep, or wanting to track politics. However, our desire can be corrupted even by good things.

While we keep God relegated to a Sunday-morning message, Americans spend an average of 8.5 hours per day engaged in "screen time."[4] In other words, we now stare at our TV's, cell phones, and

---

[4] See "Eight Hours a Day Spent on Screens, Study Finds," by Brian Stelter, New York Times (March 26, 2009)

computers for more than a third of our lives. This "screen time" is saturated with advertising designed to reach into our subconscious mind and manipulate our desires. As a result, our desires have gradually been given over to the spirit of this world. Unrestrained materialism now dominates our perspective. For some, this simply involves the desire for material things—we long to have the latest fashions, household updates, or lifestyle improvements. Others have developed such a short attention span that they need to be stimulated and entertained all the time. We have become adult babies, needing someone to coddle us, feed us, and please us at every moment. This is the exact opposite for how we are intended to live our lives. The Lord is calling us to live our lives from a much higher reality:

If then you were raised with Christ, seek those things which are above, where Christ is, sitting at the right hand of God.
Set your mind on things above, not on things on the earth.
For you died, and your life is hidden with Christ in God (Colossians 3:1-3).

The first key to freedom is recognizing who or what shapes our affections. Our goal is not to completely disengage from all media and cloister ourselves in the mountains. Our goal is to set our hearts and minds on things above, where Christ is enthroned in glory, so that we can begin to live our lives hidden in Him. For some, this pursuit may involve a period of prolonged fasting from something. However, fasting is only effective when coupled with prayer. Just like television, revelatory prayer can completely transform and shape our affections.

We can turn our faces to the Father and experience far more beauty, hope, and suspense than anything that we could possibly watch on television. When we make a deliberate choice to turn our eyes away from material things and fix our gaze on eternal things, we become connected to the ultimate source of reality. From this position, we can live our lives with desires that originate from the Holy One, so that our lives become infused with beauty, love, and joy that far exceed anything that the material world offers.

When we start to live this way, the Father reveals His perfect will for our lives. He directs us—sometimes tenderly and sometimes sternly—throughout each day so that our lives begin to be shaped and formed by Him. Through this process, the Father aligns our lives with the "scroll of destiny" already written about us in heaven.[5] We begin to receive a much greater measure of the Spirit of Holiness in our lives. The angels and the cloud of witnesses gather around us as everything in our lives will start to align with the Father's blueprints in heaven for what we are destined to become.

Look at Him Before You Jump

For those who have not yet yielded their will to the Father, the idea of completely giving ourselves to Him daily is as terrifying as looking over a precipice and being told to jump off. We usually have this feeling at first because we have not yet encountered the Father's nature. The truth is that He is a good and loving Father who wants the best for His children. When we yield our lives to Him, we do so with the confidence that He sees what is best for us much better than we can. Consider the full context of what Paul wrote when He told us to "offer our bodies as living sacrifices":

"Oh, the depth of the riches of the wisdom and knowledge of God! How unsearchable His judgments, and His paths beyond tracing out!

'Who has known the mind of the Lord? Or, who has ever been His counselor?

'Who has ever given to God, that God should repay Him?'

"For from Him and through Him and to Him are all things. To Him be the glory forever! Amen.

"Therefore, I urge you, brothers, in view of God's mercy,

---

5 See *Books of Destiny*, by Paul Keith Davis.

to offer your bodies as living sacrifices, holy and pleasing to God—this is your spiritual act of worship.

"Do not conform any longer to the pattern of this world, but be transformed by the renewing of your mind. Then, you will be able to test and approve what God's will is—His good, pleasing, and perfect will" (Romans 11:33-12:2 NIV).

Notice that Paul reminds us of the nature of God before He tells us to offer our whole being to Him. It is impossible for us to truly surrender our lives to God unless we are fully confident that He is who He says He is. Giving our bodies as "living sacrifices" is considered a "spiritual" act of worship because it proves that we truly believe what God says about Himself. In order to be willing to let go of the "pattern of this world" imprinted on our hearts and minds, we first have to have a revelation of how destructive that pattern is to ourselves and to everyone around us.

We also have to see the superiority of the heavenly pattern that the Father offers us. We are not leaping off a cliff into a dark valley of unknowing, but into the arms of the One we love and trust. David said, **"my ears you have opened"** before he said, **"I delight to do your will, my God."** We cannot truly delight in doing the will of the Father unless our spiritual eyes and ears are opened to see His superior love and wisdom.

Revelation and Longing

Our longings, affections, and desires are central to our core identity, defining who we are. When our longings, passions, and desires are changed, our core identity is fundamentally changed. The question is, what can bring about such a monumental change in us that the deepest longings in our heart—the deepest travails of our spirit—suddenly shift to what is holy and spiritual? Jesus explains what brings about this change in us:

"The kingdom of heaven is like treasure hidden in a field. When a man found it, he hid it again, and then in his joy went and sold all he had and bought that field.

"Again, the kingdom of heaven is like a merchant looking for fine pearls.

"When he found one of great value, he went away and sold everything he had and bought it" (Matthew 13:44-46 NIV).

The only way for us to be completely abandoned to God to the point that we will be willing to "sell all" is for us to first encounter the value and beauty of the kingdom of God. Unless we understand that the kingdom of God is a treasure more valuable than anything in this world, we will not be willing to "sell all" with joyful abandon. Until we glimpse the "pearl of great price"—the beauty of the Lord and the very real and magnificent splendor of His coming kingdom—we will not have the resolve to lay aside lesser pursuits.

The kingdom of God is so valuable and beautiful that it immediately instills in us a longing that is much greater than any other longing in this world. Once we have truly encountered the kingdom—once we have glimpsed the reality of the New Jerusalem and touched, tasted, and handled the glorious things in store for us—it is too late to go back. Our revelation of the kingdom grabs hold of us so firmly that we quickly lose our affections for anything else. This is why Paul said:

For it is impossible for those who were once enlightened, and have tasted the heavenly gift, and have become partakers of the Holy Spirit,
and have tasted the good word of God and the powers of the age to come,
if they fall away, to renew them again to repentance, since they crucify again for themselves the Son of God, and put Him to an open shame.
For the earth which drinks in the rain that often comes upon

it, and bears herbs useful for those by whom it is cultivated, receives blessing from God;

but if it bears thorns and briers, it is rejected and near to being cursed, whose end is to be burned (Hebrews 6:4-8).

Before we consider the negative aspects of what Paul is saying, let us look at the positive aspects. When we really taste the **"powers of the age to come,"** then we become like **"the earth which drinks in the rain . . . and bears herbs."** In other words, the most natural response for those who encounter the pleasures and revelations of the kingdom is to drink them in until we bear good spiritual fruit that is beneficial to ourselves and others.

The ones that Paul is pronouncing harsh judgment on in this passage are the people who glimpse the value and beauty of the kingdom and then continue to invest their lives in carnal pursuits. These are the people who see the kingdom but do not "drink it in" or become changed in any way. As a result of their obstinacy, they become "thorns and thistles" to everyone around them. The truth is that there are many believers—even "Spirit-filled" believers—who will be harshly judged when the Lord returns. These are the people that cannot wait to corner you so that they can tell you all the things that are wrong with the church. These are the ones who love to hide behind closed doors to share juicy morsels of gossip rooted in their own bitterness and rejection. They have glimpsed the beauty of the kingdom, only to reject it and run back to dark places.

Our Daily Walk

We often think of yielding our will to the Father as the kind of painful experience that Jesus had in Gethsemane. However, most of Christ's life did not entail that kind of misery. He was not "sweating drops of blood" and becoming "sorrowful to the point of death" every day. Most of Christ's days were marked by simple and joyful submission to the Father. He experienced the daily ecstasy of the Spirit remaining on Him because He abided in the perfect pleasure of the Father all the time. This kind of intimacy with the Father was a result of the prophetic lifestyle Jesus lived. This is why Jesus said:

"Very truly I tell you, the Son can do nothing by himself; he can do only what he sees his Father doing, because whatever the Father does the Son also does.
"For the Father loves the Son and shows him all he does. Yes, and he will show him even greater works than these, so that you will be amazed" (John 5:19-20 NIV).

"I am telling you what I have seen in the Father's presence" (see John 8:38 NIV).

Notice what an "ordinary" day was like for Jesus: He would simply do and say what the Father revealed to Him. This sounds like a ridiculously tall order. How can any of us do and say only what is revealed to us prophetically? The way that Jesus remained in perfect submission to the Father is that His core desire was dedicated completely to pleasing the Father and abiding in intimate fellowship with Him. Many people have become shipwrecked while attempting to "do only what they see the Father doing" because this became a form of spiritualized legalism for them. They want to be obedient, but they have lost the pleasure that comes from communion with the Father.

It is important to note that when we begin to live this lifestyle, no day will be the same. Some days, we may hear the Lord speak clearly about many things and our steps will be directed by the Spirit throughout the day. Other days, the Lord may speak to us about only one crucial matter on His heart. There may also be days when God is silent.

Spiritualized legalism usually sneaks into the lives of believers who seek to obey the Father without first discovering the kind of joyful communion that Jesus enjoyed with Him. Those who try to be obedient without first discovering the immense pleasure of knowing God end up spiritually bound and miserable. Our obedience should be a natural fruit of discovering a love that transcends all other loves, a beauty that transcends all earthly beauty, and a joy that surpasses any other joy. In this way, abiding in the Father's perfect will is not a religious obligation, but the natural fruit of abiding in the pleasures and glories of His eternal kingdom. Consider what Jesus said when He prayed for all of those who would believe in Him:

"My prayer is not for them alone. I pray also for those who will believe in me through their message,
"that all of them may be one, Father, just as you are in me and I am in you. May they also be in us so that the world may believe that you have sent me.
"I have given them the glory that you gave me, that they may be one as we are one—
"I in them and you in me—so that they may be brought to complete unity. Then the world will know that you sent me and have loved them even as you have loved me.
"Father, I want those you have given me to be with me where I am, and to see my glory, the glory you have given me because you loved me before the creation of the world" (John 17:20-24 NIV).

In this text, Jesus is clearly praying for every believer that will place their faith in Him throughout all the ages, not just the twelve discples or the first-century believers. Then Jesus lays out a list of core desires that He has for us.

First, Christ desires for us to be positioned "in" the Father and the Son, which speaks of a completely restored relationship between the Father, the Son, and us. The concept of being positioned "in" the Father and the Son implies that we can abide and rest in them at all times.

Second, Jesus desires for us to live in complete unity with each other. This is not a unity of politics and good intentions. When we abide in the Lord individually, then we are already on the same page and drinking the same Spirit when we come together. True unity is an expression of having the same spiritual nature.

Last, Jesus says, **"Father, I want those you have given me to be with me where I am, and to see my glory."** Verb tense is important here. Jesus did not say, "I want them to be with Me where I am going," but **"where I [presently] am."** Where was He at this moment? He was where He always was during His earthly ministry—positioned in perfect unity with the Father and abiding in His good pleasure. He was literally beholding the Father's glory at that moment and saying what He was saying.

Bringing Heaven to Earth

Yet the news about him spread all the more, so that crowds of people came to hear him and to be healed of their sicknesses.
But Jesus often withdrew to lonely places and prayed (Luke 5:15-16 NIV).

Bringing the reality of heaven to earth is the end goal of redeeming our affections and desires. Religion tells us to cloister ourselves away from the world and never return to make an impact. Jesus would often go to "withdraw to lonely places and pray" only to recharge His spiritual battery so that He could go back into society with the power to transform it.

When we begin our journey, the Father may often have us locked away for a season so to learn to truly encounter Him and access heaven. However, if we are truly hearing from Him, then we will also access His immense desire to go back out at some point and touch the lives of those around us.

Anyone who has been involved in ministry can tell you that the needs and desires of people can be overwhelming. Likewise, crowds gathered around Jesus all the time, and every person had a pressing and important need. However, Christ's response was often to withdraw and pray. This response demonstrates that Christ was completely dependent on the Father. He did not lack compassion. He simply recognized that in His earthly ministry, He could literally do nothing without the Father.

Our lives can function like the gateway to heaven at Bethel, where the angels ascended and descended. We can learn to "go up" and be with God, accessing heavenly realities. However, we also need to "go back down" and faithfully do and say what we have been shown there. The reason that many churches and ministries fall, fail, and grow weary is because they become overwhelmed with the needs of the people at the very moment that they should be "going back up" for an extended time of fresh revelation.

This same principle applies to our individual lives. God cares about our family, our home, our career, and our earthly pursuits. He knows the number of hairs on each of our heads and the number of dollars in our bank accounts. However, in order to steward our lives well, we have to live like we too are at Bethel. If we forsake our pursuit and affection for earthly things, then the Father will actually give us much more power and authority to transform the earth around us.

The Seal of Desire

Place me like a seal over your heart, like a seal on your arm; for love is as strong as death, its jealousy unyielding as the grave. It burns like a blazing fire, like a mighty flame.
Many waters cannot quench love; rivers cannot wash it away. If one were to give all the wealth of his house for love, it would be utterly scorned (Song of Songs 8:6-7 NIV84).

Our desire for Him can be so all-encompassing that it becomes like a "seal" marking everything we think, feel, and do in this life. This is a love stronger than death. For once we truly encounter the beauty of the Son of God, then we will be willing to give all to Him—even our own lives.

Religion calls us to give things up because we feel a sense of obligation or requirement. However, the seal of love compels us to give things up out of longing and desire to attain deeper communion with the Spirit. When fully revealed, this is a love that "many waters" cannot quench. This is a love that laughs at what the world offers and holds on to the revelation of perfect love with an unwavering and firm grip.

This love is a jealous love. It fully beholds the jealous desire of God to be with us. It also responds to this holy jealousy with a willingness to give all in pursuit of an even deeper level of consecration and desire. A few verses after this jealous "seal of love" is described, we find the bride declaring:

I have become in his eyes like one bringing contentment (see Song of Songs 8:10 NIV).

Once we fully yield our will to the Godhead, our striving is completely over. Instead of striving to please God through religious exercises, we are simply abiding in His perfect contentment. As those taught the fallacy of "mere salvation," we are indoctrinated to believe that we will forever remain fallen sinners, wavering between desire for the world and desire for God. However, it is possible to arrive at a place of such jealous desire for God that He becomes completely pleased and content with who we are. This is when we have learned to embody the righteousness of Christ that was legally applied to us when we were saved. This is when, having glimpsed His perfect love and desire for us at Gethsemane, we now choose to take this cup and drink it with Him, knowing full well the joy that is set before us.

The Book of Song of Songs closes with these two verses:

<u>Lover [The Bridegroom Speaking]</u>:
"You who dwell in the gardens with friends in attendance, let me hear your voice!"

<u>Beloved [The Bride Speaking]</u>:
"Come away, my lover, and be like a gazelle or like a young stag on the spice-laden mountains" (Song of Songs 8:13-14 NIV84).

Today, the Lover beckons us to speak to Him. He wants to hear our voices as much as we want to hear His. Many of us have been walking through spiritual experiences, tasting and touching the spiritual realities of the kingdom of God. We have been accompanied by angels, the cloud of witnesses, and the living saints around us—the "friends in attendance," guiding us through this spiritual journey. Now, the Lover wants these spiritual experiences to become the inspiration for a rising chorus of prayer and worship that reflects our pure longing and desire.

The new songs coming to close the gates of hell and open the gates of heaven will be songs conceived by holy desire. For nothing is powerful enough to overcome our desire for God once it is fully conceived. Instead, this desire becomes a mighty flame that consumes everything in our possession.

We must also realize that not all "songs" involve music. Many of our "songs" involve other pursuits, for anything conceived by holy desire has a distinct spiritual harmony and musical quality with the power to touch and transform lives. This is true of art, music, gardening, and parenting—even business and governmental pursuits. There will be a marked difference on everything in our lives.

Holy desire is like a small golden root that grows in us. If we nurture it, this holy desire will displace competing affections in our lives. If we allow it to grow stronger, it will align our lives with the Father so fully that His Presence marks every pursuit in our lives. This is how the rising holy ones will choose to live.

Small Group Discussion Questions

Foundation Scripture One: Song of Solomon 8:6-7

1. What are desire and love compared to in this text?

2. How does desire for God help us to yield to Him in the most difficult times of our lives?

3. Is there anything that our desire for God cannot "burn out" of our lives?

4. How does greater desire for God help us to fulfill our destiny?

Foundation Scripture Two: Romans 11:33-12:2

5. What is our "spiritual act of worship?"

6. How are Paul's instructions in Romans 12:1-2 similar to what Christ endured in Gethsemane? How are they different?

7. Are believers meant to give their lives to the Lord only once at the moment of salvation, or every day? How can daily consecration help us draw closer to the Lord?

8. What aspects of the Lord's nature must we see in order to desire to fully yield our lives to Him daily?

Cultivating a "Golden Mind" 11

If you travel through Europe's Medieval cathedrals, you will find different corpses on display in glass boxes. These are the remains of saints that the Catholic Church considers holy. These corpses are called "beatified" because their flesh appears to be uncorrupted by ordinary decay. Pilgrims still flock to these churches to view these "holy people" on display. However, for those of us who are living, holiness does not mean we reach a place of beatification where we are frozen in place as perfect saints—it means that we have dedicated ourselves to an upward journey that will never end, despite its obstacles.

In Zechariah 3, we see a remarkable symbol of our redemption. This chapter applies to us because the prophet clarified that it was **"symbolic of things to come"** (see **Zechariah 3:8**) after the Messiah was revealed. First, we see the high priest Joshua standing in filthy robes. Satan stands next to him, accusing him and pointing out his unworthy position. Then something remarkable happens:

> The Lord said to Satan, "The Lord rebuke you, Satan! The Lord, who has chosen Jerusalem, rebuke you! Is not this man a burning stick snatched from the fire?"

> Now Joshua was dressed in filthy clothes as he stood before the angel.
> The angel said to those who were standing before him, "Take off his filthy clothes." Then he said to Joshua, "See, I have taken away your sin, and I will put rich garments on you."
> Then I said, "Put a clean turban on his head." So they put a clean turban on his head and clothed him, while the angel of the Lord stood by.
> The angel of the Lord gave this charge to Joshua:
> "This is what the Lord Almighty says, 'If you will walk in my ways and keep my requirements, then you will govern my house and have charge of my courts, and I will give you a place among these standing here'" (Zechariah 3:2-7 NIV).

The first portion of this passage describes what happens when we repent and give our lives to Christ. The filthy rags of our sinful nature are stripped from us and we are bestowed with the righteousness of Christ as a legal matter. Many believers stop here, satisfied with their eternal destiny and wanting nothing more. However, the deeper streams begin one step further, where Joshua is commissioned to govern the Lord's house and serve in His heavenly courts. There are new dimensions of righteousness available to those who will commit themselves to these higher purposes. God does not clean us up to put us on display as perfect saints—He cleans us up so He can put us to work.

The most liberated people I know are those who are fully committed to doing the work of the Father. The most oppressed people I know are those who are obsessed with their own condition. This is because the Father's work always involves selfless love and service to others. When we commit ourselves to this kind of kingdom work, we lose sight of ourselves and become a channel for the Lord to work through. As we become conduits of His healing love and anointing, we ourselves become more consecrated and holy with every passing day. In contrast, those who are always navelgazing have a spirituality of self-centeredness. If we seek only to be served, we can never reach the same level of freedom, holiness, and power as those who are committed to being servants.

Cultivating a Golden Mind

The Levitical priests wore a golden crown on their forehead inscribed with the words, **"Holy to the Lord" (see Leviticus 8:9)**. The end goal is to lay hold of a thought-life made completely holy so that our minds can receive the kind of revelation that will bring the kingdom of God to earth. The goal is to cultivate a golden mind—a mind rewired by the Spirit of Holiness to the point that it becomes a conduit for receiving and transmitting heavenly realities. However, this gold crown was also positioned on a turban, a large swath of white linen wrapped around the priest's head.

When the high priest Joshua was raised up, the angel of the Lord specifically told the angels of the Lord: **"Put a clean turban on his head" (see Zechariah 3:5)**. This turban speaks of protection from every evil influence. Turbans were designed for people who live in the desert. They protect you in a sandstorm, keep you warm at night, and shield you from the sun during the day. When we are made holy, it does not only entail us being dedicated to the Lord. It also includes the Lord being dedicated to us. When we consecrate our minds to the Lord daily, we receive a new level of grace and protection allowing us to preserve the precious communion that we have with Him. Once we are His, He will shield us from many of the thoughts that compete for our attention because He is a jealous God (see Exodus 34:14).

The Sound of Oppression Leaving

I often think about what Elijah did on Mt. Horeb when he was running from Jezebel. Jezebel had terrified Elijah so much that he ran to the desert and became depressed and suicidal. In other words, Elijah's thought-life was in shambles. When the word of the Lord came to him again, Elijah was simply told to go back to the mountain. Likewise, we need to learn to go back to the mountain of the Lord whenever our thought-life falls apart. However, we see some strange things that happened on the mountain:

> Then He said, "Go out, and stand on the mountain before the Lord." And behold, the Lord passed by, and a great and strong wind tore into the mountains and broke the rocks in pieces before the Lord, but the Lord was not in the wind; and after the wind an earthquake, but the Lord was not in the earthquake;
> and after the earthquake a fire, but the Lord was not in the fire; and after the fire a still small voice.
> So it was, when Elijah heard it, that he wrapped his face in his mantle and went out and stood in the entrance of the cave. Suddenly a voice came to him… (see I Kings 19:11-13).

First, we see a strong wind, an earthquake, and a fire that the Lord was not in. This is strange because Elijah had just called down fire on Mount Carmel that the Lord was in, followed by weather patterns that broke Israel's drought—which God also caused. I interpret the wind, earthquake, and the fire on Mount Carmel to be a manifestation of the demonic powers that Elijah was facing, which were ultimately rooted in Jezebel's invocation of demons and fallen angels through idolatry. These were powers that had to leave and release their hold on Elijah as soon as he entered back into the presence of God. What we see here is their departure as they flee from the presence of the Lord. Elijah invoked this high level of deliverance through one simple act of obedience to one word from the Lord, which was to go back to the mountain.

Next, Elijah wrapped his face in his mantle. This serves the same purpose as the turban. Elijah was shielding himself from the destructive forces of the powers of darkness by wrapping all of his senses in the mantle of revelation defining his life. When he wrapped his face, he used his mantle to cover all of his senses—his eyes, ears, mouth, and nose. Likewise, when all of hell is breaking loose, we have to remember to go back up the mountain, shield all of our senses from distraction, and listen for the still small voice.

In the times of turmoil soon coming upon the earth, the Bible warns that even the abyss itself will be opened to release demonic powers not seen since before the flood (see Revelation 9). However, this same chapter also promises that these powers will not be able to harm anyone who has the seal of God (see Revelation 9:4). Until those times fall upon the world, we must make every effort to consecrate our minds to God so that we can stand up and represent Him when these times of turmoil actually come. Those who press in to find their mantle now will be able to wrap themselves in it when the times of shaking come. Instead of panicking, they will be wrapped in a mantle of transcendent peace and revelation that flows from heaven. This is the inheritance for all of the priests and prophets of the Lord. Paul explains:

When all of hell is breaking loose, we have to remember to go back up the mountain, shield all of our senses from distraction, and listen for the still small voice.

> For those who live according to the flesh set their minds on the things of the flesh, but those who live according to the Spirit, the things of the Spirit.
> For to be carnally minded is death, but to be spiritually minded is life and peace (Romans 8:5-6).

Our religious mindsets have turned this Scripture upside down. We usually associate being spiritually minded with the stress of trying to satisfy impossible religious restrictions. However, when we truly learn to yield our minds to the Spirit, then we will have a peace wrapped around our heads no matter what is happening in the world around us. We will be able to speak life to others when the world itself is trembling with turmoil. This is the hour when those who have invested their lives in spiritual things will begin to get a great return on their investment. The good news is that when this shaking comes, the children of light—the holy people—will arise and shine, giving those who are carnally minded a chance to come to the light of the Lord. Even though the ultimate fruit of a carnal mind is death, multitudes are about to be given a second chance to receive the transcendent peace and eternal life that comes from believing in Christ.

Identifying and Amplifying Spiritual Longing

"Yet a time is coming and has now come when the true worshipers will worship the Father in the Spirit and in truth, for they are the kind of worshipers the Father seeks.
"God is spirit, and his worshipers must worship in the Spirit and in truth" (John 4:23-24 NIV).

The Father is actively seeking worshipers who will worship Him **"in the Spirit and in truth."** The phrase **"in the Spirit and in truth"** in this text implies more than simply finding a balance between teaching the Bible and making room for spiritual gifts to operate in our services. The Father is looking for true worshippers—those who worship Him because their human spirit has been freed from darkness, made alive, and filled with desire for Him.

The Spirit of Holiness is looking to activate and resurrect the whole man. It is good for us to seek to align our hearts and minds with the Spirit of Holiness. However, our hearts and minds simply reflect what is happening at a much deeper level in our spirits. He causes us to long for Him with all of the romance, beauty, and devotion of a young bride. This is when we step into the spiritual reality described in the first chapter of this book:

"Wake up, sleeper, rise from the dead, and Christ will shine on you" (Ephesians 5:14 NIV).

At first, we only notice this awakening in our thought-life and emotions, for our thoughts and emotions are the mouthpieces that declare what is happening at a deeper level in the depths of our spirit. However, at some point, our spirits become so filled with the light of Christ that their unique voice will come to the surface. This may sound strange, but Paul explains:

We know that the whole creation has been groaning as in the pains of childbirth right up to the present time.
Not only so, but we ourselves, who have the firstfruits of the Spirit, groan inwardly as we wait eagerly for our adoption to sonship, the redemption of our bodies.
For in this hope we were saved. But hope that is seen is no hope at all. Who hopes for what they already have?
But if we hope for what we do not yet have, we wait for it patiently.
In the same way, the Spirit helps us in our weakness. We do not know what we ought to pray for, but the Spirit himself intercedes for us through wordless groans.
And he who searches our hearts knows the mind of the Spirit, because the Spirit intercedes for God's people in accordance with the will of God (Romans 8:22-27 NIV).

We need to recognize the unique voice of our human spirit after Christ has raised it up. Our minds speak through thoughts. These thoughts may be a series of images or an eternal dialogue depending on our thinking style. Our hearts speak through emotions and feelings. However, our spirits have a unique voice that sounds like wordless groans. These are the deeper longings from which all our thoughts and emotions spring forth.

Our spirits are like a violin string. As long as we remain lost in the outer darkness, we will have no song because our spirits are dark and sleeping. However, when the Spirit of Holiness begins to move upon our human spirit, it is like a master violinist running a bow across a Stradivarius for the first time. He awakens the song in us. He awakens the inward groaning to seek out His light, life, and love. He awakens the inner groaning to be adopted as true sons and daughters of God. He even awakens the groaning for the restoration of the earth itself.

When we yield ourselves to the Spirit of Holiness, He awakens a song in us that can completely liberate our hearts and minds from every last vestige of darkness. This is because the groaning that proceeds from our spirit comes from the eternal realm where Christ is seated, for ultimately our deepest longing is for Him. Our song comes from the reality that we are already **"seated with Christ in heavenly places" (see Ephesians 2:6).** The value in recognizing and amplifying the unique groanings in our spirit is that eventually we can allow our deepest spiritual longings to define and shape what is happening in our hearts and minds. We can subject our hearts and minds to our deep longing for God. We can allow the wordless groanings of our awakened spirit to be the song that reshapes and redefines who we are and how we live.

In the next move of God, we will see multitudes coming together to worship God. When they worship, they will literally open up the gates of heaven and close the gates of hell. This is because when they come together, it will be like the sound of 10,000 Stradivarius violins playing in harmony together. The new songs and the new sounds that are coming will be anointed with divine authority to change what is happening on the earth because these songs and sounds will proceed from the eternal realms where Christ is seated.

We often focus on the negative aspects of the great tribulation. However, we have barely glimpsed the glorious promises for this time. John prophesied:

> **And I saw what looked like a sea of glass glowing with fire and, standing beside the sea, those who had been victorious over the beast and its image and over the number of its name. They held harps given them by God**
> **and sang the song of God's servant Moses and of the Lamb** (see Revelation 15:2-3 NIV).

There will be a vast body of people who will be victorious over the beast, his image, and his number. In other words, they will have total authority over the most mature expression of evil that the earth has ever witnessed. The song of Moses and the song of the Lamb are both songs that celebrate complete deliverance, for this vast throng of people will be delivered from everything that assails them. However, this is not a deliverance from afar—it is a deliverance from within. For each one of them was given a harp, which speaks of the unique sound of longing for God and travail for heavenly realities each of us carries.

As we approach the end of the age, let us not be distracted by what the powers of darkness are doing. Let us set our full attention on what God is doing within. Our authority is ultimately derived from our connection to Christ—the communion between our own human spirit and His Spirit of Holiness. This song will erupt from all of those who are seated with Christ, seeing things from His perspective as they unfold. Let us make every effort to rosin the bow before these times unfold. Let us get in touch with our longings for heavenly beauty. Let us play each strain of the song that we have been given with poise and passion. For ultimately, this song will carry us to heights that the powers of darkness cannot reach.

A Language Beyond Words

God is beginning to speak a language to us that transcends words, thoughts, and feelings. This is a language that cannot be found in our dream interpretation manuals because it even goes beyond images and symbols. He is speaking with heavenly sounds that go much deeper than all other forms of communication. This is what John wrote about the sealed ones:

> And I heard a voice from heaven, like the voice of many waters, and like the voice of loud thunder. And I heard the sound of harpists playing their harps.
> They sang as it were a new song before the throne, before the four living creatures, and the elders; and no one could learn that song except the hundred and forty-four thousand who were redeemed from the earth (Revelation 14:2-3).

There is a transcendent song of longing, beauty, and authority that no one can learn unless they are sealed by the Lord. The reason that only the sealed ones can learn this song is because they are the only ones who are actually hearing what is happening in heaven. The song of them playing their harps is their best attempt at replicating the "voice of many waters and the voice of loud thunder" that happens in heaven all the time.

The way that we learn to "pray without ceasing" is by recognizing that the song in our own spirit is playing all the time because the song in heaven that our spirit is connected to is playing all the time. Whether we are washing dishes, changing diapers, or out on a date with our spouse, there is a harmonic vibration of our desire for God and His desire for us always thundering and rushing just beneath the surface. This is a song that hits high strains of love and pleasure and low tones of peace and gentleness, but has also been known to produce thunder and lightning that can transform the very world we live in. This is because the song that our spirits sing as believers is the same song that is always sung in heaven:

"Holy, Holy, Holy is the Lord Almighty the whole earth is full of his glory" (Isaiah 6:3 NIV).

"Holy, Holy, Holy is the Lord God Almighty who was, and is, and is to come" (Revelation 4:8 NIV).

In other words, what our spirit is declaring to our heart and mind is the distinct and higher nature of the Spirit of Holiness who abides in us. Our goal then is to develop the eyes to see and the ears to hear so that this song will emerge from the depths and find its voice in our hearts and minds.

Recognizing Anointed Thoughts

"Whenever Aaron enters the Holy Place, he will bear the names of the sons of Israel over his heart on the breastpiece of decision as a continuing memorial before the Lord.
"Also put the Urim and the Thummim in the breastpiece, so they may be over Aaron's heart whenever he enters the presence of the Lord. Thus Aaron will always bear the means of making decisions for the Israelites over his heart before the Lord" (Exodus 28:29-30 NIV).

The Urim and the Thummim were stones that lit up to help the priests make decisions for themselves or to assist the nation in making decisions. The reason the Urim and Thummim were placed in the breast piece alongside the twelve stones is because the right decisions are made in the context of having our hearts in the right place concerning God's people. In the Levitical priesthood, these twelve stones spoke of the twelve tribes of Israel that they represented and identified with. However, in the priesthood of Melchizedek, these twelve stones speak of the city of God that we are pursuing, which includes both Jews and Gentiles. This city also happens to have a foundation of twelve stones of the same precise composition as the ones in the breastplate. If the glory of this radiant city rests over our hearts continually, then it will be easier to see what decisions we should make each day as pilgrims in pursuit of it. Only those who have their "hearts set on pilgrimage" will be able to make the valley of tears a place of healing springs through the decisions that they make (see Psalm 84).

We will not always hear the Father speak in a booming voice from heaven. We will not always have a dramatic dream, vision, or trance to show us what to do. The Father wants us to be so in tune with His Spirit that we can discern which thoughts "light up" and which are dark. When we consecrate our lives to God, He places an anointing on our thought-life. This does not mean that every thought we have is from Him, but it does mean that we can grow in discernment until we recognize the mark of light and peace that rests on an anointed thought. Through daily practice, we can learn to discern the difference between our natural and normal human thoughts, anointed thoughts that come from the Spirit of God, and thoughts that are demonic in origin.

The way we make our thought-life holy is simple. We choose to reject thoughts that are demonic in origin, give our normal human thoughts their proper place, and give special consideration to the thoughts that the Spirit anoints. Initially, the process of bringing our thought-life into proper order can be challenging. This is why the Scriptures tell us:

For though we live in the world, we do not wage war as the world does.
The weapons we fight with are not the weapons of the world. On the contrary, they have divine power to demolish strongholds.

> We demolish arguments and every pretension that sets itself up against the knowledge of God, and we take captive every thought to make it obedient to Christ (II Corinthians 10:3-5 NIV).

Paul is using the aggressive language of war here. However, he is not talking about an external battle. He is talking about the internal battle that happens in our thought-life. In order to become the holy people that we are called to be, we first have to "demolish" the strongholds in our minds. These strongholds are the lies and arguments that we believe. They are torn down by simply recognizing the truth of God's Word—our primary weapon. For example, someone who frequently uses pornography believes the internal argument that they have to use it because they cannot be fulfilled without it. Someone who suffers from rejection believes the internal argument that they are unloved by God or by others. Someone who is depressed often believes the argument that their joy is defined by circumstances. Every war that rages in our mind can ultimately be traced to an erroneous internal argument that keeps us in bondage. Some of these arguments can be dismantled simply by reading and believing what the Bible says about us. However, most of these strongholds must be intentionally dismantled by seeking out the "higher thoughts" of God that have the power to dismantle, displace, and deconstruct our "lower thoughts." For the Lord has said:

> "For My thoughts are not your thoughts, nor are your ways My ways," says the Lord.
> "For as the heavens are higher than the earth, so are My ways higher than your ways, and my thoughts than your thoughts" (Isaiah 55:8-9).

It is important to realize that even in the midst of significant battles for freedom in our thought-life, we can always "escape up" to access the eternal realm where Christ is seated. Often, the things that we cannot defeat in our own strength by wrestling, Christ will defeat with His real and tangible presence if we seek Him first. We need to learn to "go up" at the moments when we normally "give up." God offers a path of holiness to every one of us that no evil thought is permitted to touch. This is a path marked out by holy and anointed thoughts designed to bring us to a fuller understanding of who God is and who we are in Him.

When we deal with demonic strongholds, we often follow "trails" of thoughts into dark places. This is why we need to train ourselves to take the first thought captive—for we usually already know where it will lead us. However, the same is true about the way of holiness. If we engage the first anointed thought that the Spirit gives us, then we soon find another and another. Just like a runway that is lit up at night for planes to take off, we can follow anointed thoughts right up into a new way of thinking by dwelling on the things that God's mind is dwelling on.

The Full Expanse of Our Priestly Authority

The tongue has the power of life and death, and those who love it will eat its fruit (Proverbs 18:21 NIV).

The Scriptures are clear that our tongues have the power to "steer the ship" or "light a forest on fire." We have power to guide and bless others on their journey—or bring great destruction—through what we speak. Over the past few decades, the Lord has sent many great teachers to highlight the importance and power of our words. As a new believer, I was drawn to the writings of Charles Capps, who emphasized the power of declaration. I quickly found that when I avoided negative words, refrained from gossip or backbiting, and used my tongue to bless others, the Lord granted new authority to what I prayed and declared. This is because God can trust a restrained tongue. However, our priestly authority extends far beyond mere words.

God does not anoint the tongue only, but the whole person. If we yield to the Spirit of Holiness in what we say, we will be given more authority in our declarations because God can trust us. Many believers over the last few decades have heard and internalized the message that we must discipline our tongues in this way. However, this same principle can be applied to our thoughts, our emotions, and our imaginations.

What would happen if we applied this same discipline to our thoughts, emotions, and imaginations? What if we refused to even think, feel, or imagine anything negative about ourselves or others? What if instead of letting our carnal minds wander, we yielded them fully to the Spirit of Holiness and asked Him to anoint our thought-life, so that we can think His thoughts, feel His burdens, and glimpse His vision for ourselves and others? The end result of this discipline is we become holy vessels who carry much more anointing and authority—not only in what we say, but in who we are becoming.

Remember, the priests were not dressed only in white robes, which represented righteous deeds (see Revelation 19:8). As discussed earlier, the priests also wore a golden crown over their turban etched with the words, "Holiness Unto the Lord." God is calling us to consecrate our minds as holy. We have the opportunity to surrender our thought-life to Him so fully that we become conduits for receiving His thoughts and transmitting them to others through intercession, prophecy, and evangelism. This does not mean that every thought we will have will be from God—we will still have to exercise discernment. However, it means we are choosing to position ourselves as a lightning rod for whenever He is looking to move on the earth. The best way to rewire our minds to become God's lightning rods is to truly learn to **"love one another deeply, from the heart"** (see I Peter 1:22 NIV).

The Journey of Exploring God's Thoughts

The thoughts of God are so breathtakingly beautiful and captivating that I can't imagine why anyone would not want to spend their entire life exploring them. The most remarkable thing about God's thoughts is that they involve us personally. David declared:

How precious to me are your thoughts, O God! How vast the sum of them!
Were I to count them, they would outnumber the grains of sand (see Psalm 139:17-18 NIV).

What did David find so precious about God's thoughts? Why was he so utterly captivated by them? The context of this Scripture makes it clear. Just before David said this, he explained how the thoughts of God concerned him personally:

You have searched me, Lord, and you know me.
You know when I sit and when I rise; you perceive my thoughts from afar.
You discern my going out and my lying down; you are familiar with all my ways.
Before a word is on my tongue you, Lord, know it completely.
You hem me in behind and before, and you lay your hand upon me.
Such knowledge is too wonderful for me, too lofty for me to attain.
Where can I go from your Spirit? Where can I flee from your presence?
If I go up to the heavens, you are there; if I make my bed in the depths, you are there.
If I rise on the wings of the dawn, if I settle on the far side of the sea,
even there your hand will guide me, your right hand will

hold me fast.

If I say, "Surely the darkness will hide me and the light become night around me,"

even the darkness will not be dark to you; the night will shine like the day, for darkness is as light to you.

For you created my inmost being; you knit me together in my mother's womb.

I praise you because I am fearfully and wonderfully made; your works are wonderful, I know that full well.

My frame was not hidden from you when I was made in the secret place, when I was woven together in the depths of the earth.

Your eyes saw my unformed body; all the days ordained for me were written in your book before one of them came to be.

How precious to me are your thoughts, O God! How vast the sum of them!

Were I to count them, they would outnumber the grains of sand (Psalm 139:1-18 NIV).

Notice the spiritual realities that David describes here. He became aware of God's presence enveloping every aspect of his life, from his very conception until the present day. He describes how God is completely "familiar" with every aspect of his life. He is overwhelmed by the revelation that he is "hemmed in" on every side by the inescapable presence of God. This describes what it feels like to walk in the Highway of Holiness. You won't be able to go anywhere without God. Whether you're encountering the darkest forces that hell can unleash or you're discovering the glorious beauty of heaven itself, God is right there with you, bombarding you with His endless love, beauty, and sustaining Spirit. Once you begin walking in the thoughts of God concerning your life, it is like discovering the most romantic lover imaginable. I cannot imagine why anyone would want to get off this road.

The restoration of our thought-life does not begin with constant ministry towards others, but with a pure revelation of what God thinks about us. Revelation of God's desire for us personally brings revelation of His love crashing over our thoughts and emotions like ocean waves. The painful chapters of our life are changed and beautified by His surrounding presence until we find ourselves adrift on an ocean of His love. God wants all of us to experience this kind of intimacy and restoration personally so we can minister to others out of the overflow of a "full cup" of love. This is why Paul prayed that we would be **"rooted and established in love"** until we understand its full **"height and width and depth"** (see Ephesians 3:16-19).

If we are properly "rooted" in love, then we will be so firmly planted in the heart of God that we will not be uprooted when the heavy winds of rejection, accusation, or offense come. Instead of being pulled into the darkness of anger and resentment, we will be quick to love and forgive others because our roots are sunk deep into the heart of God.

Walking the Beach with the Lord

About three years ago, I had a vision where I was walking with the Lord on a beach. The beach was breathtakingly beautiful and extended infinitely into the mists in front of us. I felt His captivating love for me as He said:

"My thoughts are as endless as the sands on this beach. You can access as many of them as you choose to as long as you walk with Me. And My glory is like the waves on this ocean. Wave after wave, I will allow My Spirit to break over your life until you are conformed to My nature."

As He said this, I felt regret for how little I have sought His thoughts or His Spirit. I longed to remain there with Him. I wept under the weight of love I felt as He said this and felt a burning desire to seek Him more, to truly know His thoughts and walk in His ways.

Then, I started to ask Him about people in my life that I've been praying for—especially those who I did not really know or understand. He picked up a seashell, at which point I noticed that many seashells were washing up on the shore. Then He said,

"I will only reveal to you what I will do in other people's lives to the extent that you love them as I do."

As soon as He said this, I realized that the shells represented prophetic clarity about the people I was interceding for. He would give me the revelation to hold those in my hands who I would commit to love as He loves.

I also believe there is a hidden message in this parable. As we walked, there were more and more shells washing up on the beach until it was almost covered. There are many people who have been in God's "breakers" for a long time but are about to land in the infinite expanse of God's thoughts. The glorious truth about the intercession, prophecy, and evangelism is that we can become God's conduits for transmitting His thoughts to others.

Since I had this revelation of the beach, I have had plenty of time to test what the Lord showed me. I have found that this strategy actually works. If I cannot see or sense anything to pray for someone, then I search my heart to make sure that I am loving them as God does. Once I learn to love them, then it becomes an easy matter to see the Father's perfect will for their life and declare that it be done. This journey begins with prayer, but if we truly capture God's heart for others, we will also be driven to tell them what He is thinking about them.

SMALL GROUP DISCUSSION QUESTIONS

Foundation Scripture One: Zechariah 3:1-10

1. Describe Joshua's spiritual state before the Lord redeemed him. (What was he wearing? What was he hearing and seeing?)

2. Describe Joshua's spiritual state after the Lord redeemed him. (What was he wearing? What was he hearing and seeing?)

3. As a priest of the Lord, what did Joshua have full access to as soon as he was redeemed?

4. What was Joshua commissioned for in verse 7?

5. How does this chapter relate to our own transformation and preparation for service as a "royal priesthood" under the New Covenant (see I Peter 2:9)?

Foundation Scripture Two: I Kings 19:1-13

6. What kind of spiritual attack was Elijah facing in the first half of this chapter?

7. Who was behind the spiritual attack against Elijah? How did it affect his mind, will, and emotions?

8. Where did Elijah have to return to in order to "rise above" the spiritual assault he was facing?

9. What did Elijah do to shield his senses? What can we do to wrap our faces in the peace of God and hear from Him when spiritual attacks come?

10. Release God's peace and the spirit of prophecy over all those present at the meeting. Make proclamations inspired by Zechariah 3 and I Kings 19.

The Rise of His Living Lightnings 12

Enoch spoke one of the greatest promises of the Bible when he declared,

"The Lord is coming with thousands upon thousands of his holy ones

"to judge everyone, and to convict all of them of all the ungodly acts they have committed in their ungodliness, and of all the defiant words ungodly sinners have spoken against him" (Jude 1:14-15 NIV).

Enoch's words do not prophesy that a holy people will arise who condemns everyone else. Rather, his words proclaim the rise of a holy people who will bring conviction. Although they will speak the words given to them with boldness, this conviction will not come primarily from words, but from the great light of the Spirit of Holiness radiating from their being.

The best way to understand the impact of this holy people is to go back to Jesus' instructions in the Sermon on the Mount:

"You are the salt of the earth. But if the salt loses its saltiness, how can it be made salty again? It is no longer good for anything, except to be thrown out and trampled underfoot.

"You are the light of the world. A town built on a hill cannot be hidden.

"Neither do people light a lamp and put it under a bowl. Instead they put it on its stand, and it gives light to everyone in the house.

"In the same way, let your light shine before others, that they may see your good deeds and glorify your Father in heaven" (Matthew 5:13-16 NIV).

These rising holy ones will be the people who actually become the salt and light Jesus calls us to be. They will bring conviction, redemption, and restoration to everyone and everything in their sphere of influence by the simple virtue of who they are. Just as salt preserves meat, the neighborhoods, regions, and nations where these holy ones rise will be preserved from destruction. Just as a lamp dispels darkness, the fear, anxiety, hatred, and lawlessness that proceeds from the powers of darkness will not be able to take root in any place where they are standing as lampstands.

About the Following Section

As I finished this book, I was strongly prompted to remind the reader of some of Enoch's specific prophecies for our generation. Although this section may stand alone as an affirming voice to the promises of canon Scripture, my previous books, *Enoch's Blessing* and *Paths of Ever-Increasing Glory*, explain the legitimacy and importance of Enoch's writings with more detail.

Enoch's Prophecy for the Righteous (Enoch 58)

"(1) And I began to declare the third prophecy
concerning the righteous and chosen:
(2) You are blessed,
you righteous and elect,
because your inheritance is glorious.

(3) The righteous will live
in the light of the sun,
and the chosen in
the light of eternal life:
the days of their life will never end,
and the days of these holy people
will be beyond comprehension.

(4) And they will search for light
and find righteousness in the Lord of Spirits:
there will be peace upon the righteous
in the name of the Eternal Lord.

(5) And after this, it will be said
to the holy in heaven
that they should seek out
the secrets of righteousness,
the heritage of faith:
for it has become as bright as the sun
upon the earth,
and the darkness is past.

(6) And there will be a light that never ends,
and they will never come to an end of days,
for the darkness will be destroyed first,
And the light established
in the Presence of the Lord of Spirits
and the light of honor
will be established forever
before the Lord of Spirits."

Enoch described a final generation who would "live in the light of the sun" (Enoch 58:3). He prophesied that "the days of these holy people will be beyond comprehension" (Enoch 58:3). This is also what Paul implied when he wrote, "No eye has seen, no hear has heard, no mind has conceived what God has prepared for those who love Him—but God has revealed it to us by His Spirit" (see I Corinthians 2:9-10). In other words, the level of light and power soon to rise upon God's holy ones will far exceed anything we can comprehend right now.

Enoch also tells us how these will access this high level of light and holiness: "they will search for light and find righteousness in the Lord" and they will "seek out the secrets of righteousness" (Enoch 58:4-5). In other words, they will walk in ever-increasing light because they are continually and actively seeking for it. This shows that real holiness does not begin with legalistic perfectionism, but with spiritual hunger. Jesus confirmed the words of Enoch's prophecy when He proclaimed, **"Blessed are the meek, for they will inherit the earth. Blessed are those who hunger and thirst for righteousness, for they will be filled"** (Matthew 5:5-6).[1]

The great restoration of the earth will come through a humble people hungering for righteousness until they are filled. Apart from the Spirit of Holiness, the spirit of man is a dead grey thing. However, when the Spirit of Holiness breathes upon this final generation and fills them with righteousness, we will see new levels of supernatural ministry and spiritual awakening for which we currently have no frame of reference.

Supernatural Ministry

Based on the promises of Scripture, I believe these are the kinds of supernatural ministry to be restored when the Lord raises up this holy people:

1. Priests in the Order of Melchizedek

The Melchizedek priesthood is a body of priests who transcend the realm of time-space because they are **"seated in the eternal realms with Christ"** (see Ephesians 2:6). Their basic function is to hear and see what is happening in heaven so they may declare and release it on the earth. Their home is in heaven, so their eyes are ever fixed on "**things above, where they are hidden with Christ in God**" (see **Colossians 1:1-3**). Their job is to sense everything in the Father's heart and search out the Scriptures so that they can call forth the fulfillment of His promises. They are granted limitless power and authority derived entirely from Christ's sacrifice—and not from any virtue of their own.

2. Living Witnesses

"**You will receive power when the Holy Spirit comes on you; and you will be my witnesses**" (see Acts 1:8 NIV).

We will also see a restoration of the great spiritual power that qualifies us to be Christ's witnesses. The power demonstrated in the first-century church was released during the season of the "early rains" referred to by the prophet Joel (see Joel 2). This means that everything recorded in the Book of Acts and in Paul's Epistles was a mere foretaste of the greater glory to be revealed in the "latter rains" at the end of the age.

In the New Testament, we find encounters of believers being translated from one place on the earth to another in powerful supernatural ministry. We find accounts of believers prophesying and experiencing heavenly places as John and Paul did when they saw the heavenly Jerusalem. As we enter into the time of the "latter rains," we should not be surprised if this kind of supernatural ministry becomes much more common among believers, especially because there will be many more believers stepping into the reality of the advancing kingdom of heaven.

In my previous book, *Paths of Ever-Increasing Glory*, I laid out a theology for ministry from the cloud of witnesses in the first chapter. I believe many saints are actively ministering from their position in the cloud of witnesses today. However, what if

God were to raise up "living witnesses" like Enoch? What if He were to raise up a generation of holy people who walked with the Holy One so closely that they began to live as angels, being translated from place to place to do heaven's bidding? What if they became so planted in the eternal realms that they could even traverse backwards and forwards in time to do the Father's will? As outlandish as these thoughts may sound, this may only scratch the surface of what it means for God to do something beyond what "mind can conceive." My goal is not to create a rigid theology about these things, but to present these as possibilities based on the record of Scripture to raise the ceiling on our expectations. Our lives are called to be a testimony of God's supernatural power, for the Father has said,

"You are My witnesses," says the Lord, "And My servant whom I have chosen, that you may know and believe Me, and understand that I am He. Before Me there was no God formed, nor shall there be after Me.
"I, even I, am the Lord, and besides Me there is no savior."
"I have declared and saved, I have proclaimed, and there was no foreign god among you; therefore you are My witnesses," says the Lord, "that I am God.
"Indeed before the day was, I am He; and there is no one who can deliver out of My hand; I work, and who will reverse it?" (Isaiah 43:10-13)

Based on Christ's words in the Book of Acts, our primary witness is, "**besides** [Christ] **there is no savior**" (see Isaiah 43:11)—preaching the message of "**Christ and Him crucified**" (see I Corinthians 2:2) must always remain our highest goal. Therefore, the primary reason God will raise up living witnesses is to bring the hope of the Gospel to the ends of the earth.

There are also hidden truths in this passage. The same witnesses that Christ promised to anoint with power will also "know and believe Him"—they will not only learn to preach Him, but to know Him intimately. As a result this intimate friendship, they will be raised up as "witnesses . . . that Jehovah is God" in a time when the nations are shaking and crying out for answers.

3. Brothers of Christ

> For whom He foreknew, He also predestined to be conformed to the image of His Son, that He might be the firstborn among many brethren.
> Moreover whom He predestined, these He also called; whom He called, these He also justified; and whom He justified, these He also glorified (Romans 8:29-30).

In this passage, justification refers to our salvation, when we are "justified" before the Father by placing our faith in Christ. However, the Bible here describes the next level of our Christian walk as "glorification." This refers to the rest of our Christian walk, when we are called to move from glory to glory as we drink in different aspects of who Christ is.

This final generation will mature to the point that they become completely "glorified," meaning they will be **"conformed to the image of His Son."** They will take on His divine nature by walking in His love, yielding to the will of the Father, and allowing the Spirit to direct their lives. As a result, Christ will have many "brothers and sisters" in the earth. This does not mean that we will become God. This means that we will become holy vessels God can trust with the same kind of power and authority He granted Jesus. However, Jesus suggested these would walk in much more power, for He was only the first fruits offering of a much greater restoration to come:

> **"Very truly I tell you, whoever believes in me will do the works I have been doing, and they will do even greater things**

than these, because I am going to the Father" (John 14:12 NIV).

Notice that Jesus explained these greater works would happen because He was going to the Father. This is because the release of ministry gifts and offices could not happen until "**He ascended on high . . . and gave gifts to men**" (see Ephesians 4:8). Jesus is still standing as High Priest, sprinkling the blood He shed, and praying for you to rise to a new level of holiness so you can become the vessel He will use to advance His kingdom in the earth.

The last verse of Enoch chapter 58 proclaims that the light of the Lord will be "established" permanently in the earth. Ultimately, this speaks of the restoration of all things that will occur when Christ returns.

Living Lightnings—Chapter 59

There is a last calling Enoch prophesied that seems even more outlandish than the others I described. The Lord will soon raise up an army of "living lightnings" on the earth. These will be people so yielded to heaven that they become great conduits through which the Word of the Lord can be released with great power to destroy the works of darkness and raise up the kingdom of heaven. Enoch proclaimed about this generation:

> "(1) In those days, my eyes saw
> the secrets of the lightnings,
> and of the lights,
> and the judgments that they execute:
> and they strike for a blessing "
> "or a curse as the Lord of Spirits wills.
>
> (2) And there I saw
> the secrets of the thunder,

and how when it resounds above in the heaven,
the sound of it is heard,
and He allowed me to see the judgments
being released on the earth,
whether they were for well-being and blessing,
or for a curse according to the Word
of the Lord of Spirits.

(3) And after that all the secrets
of the lights and lightnings
were shown to me:
they strike for blessing and are fulfilled."

The living lightnings Enoch describes are holy people who "strike" with blessing, prophetic declaration, prayer, preaching, evangelism, and signs and wonders whenever it thunders in heaven. This is because these holy people are fully connected to what is happening in heaven all the time. They are faithful to declare words of rebuke and bind the powers of darkness, which I believe is what is implied when Enoch proclaims they will sometimes "strike for a curse." However, their greatest fulfillment comes in the last verse, where they "strike for blessing and are fulfilled." As priests in the order of Melchizedek, the greatest power we have been given is the power to bless others with the words that heaven gives us.

In an earlier chapter of Enoch's book, he described the same courtroom scene Daniel saw in Daniel 7, where the Ancient of Days takes His seat and opens the books surrounded by a multitude of saints (see Daniel 7 and Enoch 14). This final generation will be given unprecedented access to this courtroom—until they are able

> *As priests in the order of Melchizedek, the greatest power we have been given is the power to bless others.*

to read the words in the books clearly. *This will enable them to declare them on the earth.* They will be seated in holy counsel with the Holy One because they will spend their days walking with Him. Enoch proclaimed about those who will be given access to God's courtroom:

"And the most holy ones who were near Him did not leave by night or withdraw from His Presence" (Enoch 14:23).

Instead of "leaving by night" and "withdrawing from His Presence" when the foundations of the earth are crumbling, this vast body of rising holy people will remain in His Presence all the time. As a result, they will learn ancient wisdom and revelation that no other generation could see clearly. This will enable them to have limitless power and authority as lightnings from heaven. When the Father thunders with a new judgment against the powers of darkness, these holy people will already have a decisive answer flowing like fire from their mouths. When the sea of humanity is tossed and broken by the shaking of the foundations of the earth, they will have the words of blessing that will restore the heart of man and call forth the restoration of all things.

Consider the prophetic authority John describes being given to the two witnesses in Revelation:

These are the two olive trees and the two lampstands standing before the God of the earth.
And if anyone wants to harm them, fire proceeds from their mouth and devours their enemies. And if anyone wants to harm them, he must be killed in this manner.
These have power to shut heaven, so that no rain falls in the days of their prophecy; and they have power over waters to turn them to blood, and to strike the earth with all plagues, as often as they desire (Revelation 11:4-6).
Most scholars connect this passage to Moses and Elijah. Moses was used by God to perform great signs and wonders and

bring judgment on Egypt through plagues at a time when God's people needed deliverance. Likewise, Elijah called forth fire from heaven when the whole land was in drought because the powers of darkness had possessed the land, the people, and their leaders. Others have speculated that one of the two witnesses may be Enoch because Enoch and Elijah are the only two prophets whom the Bible tells us never experienced death.

Although I am not ruling out the reappearance of Moses, Elijah, or Enoch in the future, I believe the primary purpose of this passage is to build our faith for much greater prophetic authority. We are entering a time when we will need deliverers to confront Pharaoh. We will need prophets to confront Jezebel. We will need those who walk with God to confront fallen angels. The only ones qualified to do these tasks will be those who allow themselves to be conduits of the Spirit of Holiness until they become living lightnings.

SMALL GROUP DISCUSSION QUESTIONS

Foundation Scripture One: Matthew 5:13-16

1. According to verse 16, how do people "see our light?"

2. What kinds of "good deeds" does this verse refer to? Are these works of charity, signs and wonders, healings, spiritual gifts, or something else?

3. Do you have any gifts you are "hiding under a basket" right now? If so, what can you do to set them on a stand and shine?

Foundation Scripture Two: Zechariah 4, Revelation 11:4-6

4. What is the connection between the two witnesses in Zechariah 4 and the two witnesses in Revelation 11?

5. Do you believe the Scriptures clearly indicate who the "two witnesses" are? Why or why not?

6. Could the two witnesses point to a level of prophetic authority we are meant to walk in as the end times unfold? Explain your thinking.

7. How can each of us become more powerful witnesses for the Lord? How can we become more like "golden pipes" pouring out the oil of consecration on others?

The Terror of the Holiness of the Glory   13

We are about to enter a chapter in history that every prophet and holy person longed to be a part of. This is a season when the whole world will witness unmistakable manifestations of God's glory. The greatest promise to unfold will be the second coming of Christ. His return will be the capstone—the final event—in a long series of events that fully restores His bride to be pure, glorious, and victorious.

The Scriptures proclaim the end times will be marked by "rising glory" upon God's people and "greater glory" filling His house (see Isaiah 60:1-3 and Haggai 2:6-9). In other words, God's manifest presence and power will greatly increase as we step into the end times. Trusted prophets such as Bob Jones and John Paul Jackson predicted unprecedented demonstrations of God's presence and power as we enter this new chapter—with a resurgence of resurrections, a literal return of the "glory cloud" to God's people, translations, creative miracles, and a biblical level of prophetic accuracy. However, this "greater glory" is not something that only believers will witness, for it will be one of primary things driving multitudes into the kingdom of heaven. Isaiah prophesied:

> Every valley shall be exalted and every mountain and hill brought low; the crooked places shall be made straight and the rough places smooth. The glory of the Lord shall be revealed, and all flesh shall see it together (Isaiah 40:5).

There is a clear order to how God's glory will be revealed to "all flesh" in the end times. First, His glory will "exalt every valley" as the Father heals broken lives with His glorious presence and power. This includes the salvation of a "multitude of souls" from "every tribe, tongue, and nation," as well as the unprecedented movement of signs, wonders, and miracles predicted by Scripture (see Revelation 7:9 and Joel 2). This move of God will be an event "all flesh sees together" because it will touch every nation on earth. However, this movement of "glory and harvest" is only one side of the coin of the end times. The other side of the coin is marked "judgment and shaking." We must prepare for both sides of the coin to be revealed.

The rising glory will also bring an unprecedented level of judgment upon the powers of darkness and shaking to the kingdoms of this world. In nearly every place in Scripture where this end-times glorification is discussed, we also see a prediction of great shaking happening in the world. Haggai tells us "everything that can be shaken will be shaken" just before the greater glory returns. Isaiah warns us that "deep darkness" will be upon the peoples of the earth at the time when "rising glory" appears over us (see Isaiah 60:1-3). Likewise, Peter and Paul contrasted the "glory that will be revealed" with our "present sufferings" (see Romans 8:18; I Peter 4:13, and I Peter 5:1)

There is a clear reason why shaking and glory naturally go together throughout Scripture. Shaking is used to remove obstacles to God's habitation in His people so the glory can take full root in us. Shaking is used to break the kingdoms of this world so the kingdom of God can spread throughout the earth when it reaches full maturity.

The first shaking to happen will be in us. It is good for us to be aware of the fact that God will judge and remove every power of darkness from the earth. However, His first priority is to remove every influence of the powers of darkness from within our own hearts and minds.

When the Ark Sets Out

Throughout the Scriptures, the Ark of the Covenant represents the manifest presence, power, and glory of God. The Ark rested in the Most Holy Place, the deepest and most secret chamber of the temple, because our highest calling is to abide in God's presence continually until we become the literal resting place for His glory. Therefore, the first place we should look for the "rising glory" is in our private prayer lives. One of the most neglected promises of Scripture is that we have access to "ever-increasing glory" right now through our relationship with Jesus Christ. The level of glory we carry is simply based on how much we hunger for God and press in to know Him each day.

When it's Time to Take the Land

In ancient Israel, the Ark of the Covenant did not always remain hidden in the Most Holy Place. In a time of peace, the tabernacle of Moses remained stationary and the Ark remained in a hidden place. However, in a time of war, such as when Israel marched out to take the Promised Land, the Ark of the Covenant was taken out of hiding and placed at the front of the armies of the Lord. From this vantage point, it could clearly be seen by all of Israel and her enemies. This is what will happen when we march out of the "seeker's revival" season, when God's glory is revealed in secret, and into the season of "manifest glory."

When Moses was communing with God in the Most Holy Place, he enjoyed an intimate friendship with the Lord: "**the Lord spoke to Moses face to face, as a man speaks to his friend**" (see Exodus 33:11). This intimate love and friendship with God is the foundation for all that follows. However, the glory has a much different effect when the seasons change and it is time to "take the land." The Scriptures tell us what Moses declared when it was time for the armies of God to march out with the Ark of God at the helm of their companies:

The cloud of the Lord was over them by day when they set out from the camp.
Whenever the ark set out, Moses said, "Rise up, O Lord!
May your enemies be scattered; may your foes flee before you!" (Numbers 10:35 NIV)

We see a strange dichotomy to God's glory. God's glory is synonymous with His perfect love, His wisdom, and His power. His glory heals the most broken parts of our nature and satisfies our thirst. However, this same glory is terrifying to the powers of darkness because it carries the perfection of love and holiness. The powers of darkness cannot stand in the light of perfect love because it stands in opposition to their core nature. The powers of darkness cannot handle the "beauty of holiness" because it stands in opposition to the chaotic darkness they carry. This perfection of beauty, love, and holiness is something that no power of darkness will be able to oppose once it is fully revealed. This is why Jehoshaphat appointed worshippers equipped to "**praise the beauty of holiness**" (see II Chronicles 20:21) when Israel marched out to face the enemy's forces.

The Returning Glory Cloud

When the cloud of the Lord's glory returns to the body of Christ, it will certainly bring a revelation of His great love. For even on the mountain where the Law was given, Moses heard the Lord proclaim that He is "compassionate, gracious, and rich in love" (see Exodus 34:6 NIV). God's glory will always remain an outward expression of His love because "God is love" (see I John 4:16). Much of the healing and deliverance we need will be imparted through an impartation of God's love. However, there is much more the returning glory will accomplish and reveal.

The returning glory will restore the revelations that "God is holy" and "Our God is a consuming fire, a jealous God" (see Leviticus 19:2; Deuteronomy 4:24; and Hebrews 12:29). These aspects of the returning glory are what I call, *"the terror of the holiness of the glory."* When a revelation of God's love comes out of the glory cloud, we are more likely to weep with joy or laugh as God restores the most broken places of our nature. However, when the pure holiness of God is revealed, it will fill us with a holy terror that will lead us to deeper wisdom, consecration, and fear of the Lord. Although this experience might sound terrifying, it truly is what we need to fulfill our purpose on earth. As the end times unfold, we will have many more reasons to fear man and many more temptations to compromise our love and consecration to the Lord. The purpose of the terror of the holiness of the glory is to fully establish the fear of the Lord in us so that we cannot be shaken or tempted by anything else.

When the Ark set out, Moses proclaimed God's enemies would be scattered. However, **"Whenever it came to rest, he said, 'Return, O Lord, to the countless thousands of Israel'" (see Numbers 10:35-36).** Our God is going to return to us, visiting us in dramatic displays of His power and glory. We will experience His love, His holiness, His friendship, and His terror. Those who fully embrace every aspect of God's nature will be the rising holy ones of these times. Everything they set their hands to will succeed.

When God imparts His love, it "raises up the valleys" by ministering to the hurting and broken and drawing us into deeper communion with God. However, when the "terror of the holiness of the glory" is revealed, it will "lay low the mountains." Any person, power, or mindset standing in opposition to what God wants to do in His body—or in the earth—will be greatly humbled by the coming manifestations of God's glory.

When the Philistines captured the Ark of the Covenant, the glory proceeding from the Ark that demolished their idol, afflicted the whole region with rats, and brought deadly tumors (cancer) to all the surrounding towns and villages (see I Samuel chapters 5 and 6). This is a biblical warning for anyone seeking to use God's glory to further a human agenda. Even when the Ark was returned along with "five golden tumors and five golden rats" as a guilt offering, seventy of the Israelites were struck dead because they looked into the glory apart from God's priestly model of worship and consecration (see I Samuel 6). This is a warning for anyone who takes God's glory lightly. The glory is not returning to entertain us or simply embellish our seeker-sensitive services. The glory is returning to clearly reveal God's perfect holiness, so that we will learn to **"Be holy as He is holy"** (see Leviticus 11:45). This is a holiness that will allow us to commune with the Lord, submit to His headship over our lives, and fully consecrate ourselves to Him.

Rising Water Levels of Glory, Holiness, and Consecration

As I have prayed into what the Father has prepared for us in the next few years, I saw a recurring vision of "rising water levels" of glory, holiness, and consecration. The Lord showed me the "terror of the holiness of the glory" returning in stages, with each manifestation of His glory leading us into renewed repentance, holiness, and consecration. Since I am planted at MorningStar, I saw this unfolding at different places on the

Heritage International Ministries' campus, although I believe this kind of move of the Spirit will unfold similarly at many places throughout the earth.

First, I saw the glory of the Lord returning as fine mists of different colors every day to the worshippers, prophets, and intercessors gathered at MorningStar's Bob Jones Vision Center. These mists that came revealed different aspects of God's nature so that we could drink them in and embody them. These were corporate revelations given to everyone at the same time instead of individual revelations. In this "mists" stage, the revelation that people received in visions, dreams, words, and signs from God synchronized more than ever before. People started to know what would happen in a meeting long before they arrived, and there was an unprecedented unity in the prayer and worship because of it. The corporate gatherings began to take on a light, power, and glory that shone like a beacon of hope in a time of shaking.

The other aspect of this vision happened in a much larger gathering in MorningStar's Atrium. It was here that the "terror of the holiness of the glory" was most clearly revealed. It is hard to describe the feeling that filled the room, except that the terror of God brought a delight beyond comprehension. No one could stand because of the glory or the holiness it carried. The terror of encountering God directly was not like the crippling fear we experience in our sufferings—it was the delightful terror of knowing for certain that *"Our God is right here in this room to meet with us."*

In this vision, the Father counseled every heart in how to respond to His glory. Some wept with joy and dove deeper into the mysteries of His love. Others crumbled to the floor in repentance and renewed consecration. Others felt power surging through their body as cancers and broken body parts were supernaturally healed from the glory. For about ten minutes, no one could rise or speak on the platform—until a young woman broke the silence by allowing the Father to sing His words through her. I do not interpret this vision to be a single meeting, but rather the inauguration of a new era in which the "rising glory" will be fully revealed.

If God were to show up the way we want Him to right now, we would probably face the same fate as the seventy Israelite farmers who were struck dead in the field when the Ark returned. God mercifully demonstrates the level of glory that we can handle at our current level of holiness and consecration. This is why those who seek the Lord in secret are currently experiencing much more of God's glory than is being revealed publicly. However, there is a Catch-22 here—for only the manifest glory of God can lead us to the level of holiness and consecration we need. We must look over the precipice of God's holiness and simply jump into it, beginning our transition to be the "holy ones" He dreams about. Once we commit to Him, there is no going back.

Small Group Discussion Questions

Foundation Scripture: Isaiah 40:5

1. Describe what will be different in our lives when the glory of God is revealed in greater ways.

2. What valleys do you think will be "raised up" as the Lord reveals His glory? What mountains do you think will be "laid low?"

3. How will the returning glory impact the body of Christ?

4. How will the returning glory impact the unsaved?

5. Dedicate the rest of this group session to prayers of consecration and songs of worship. Resolve to make your group a "resting place for the glory of God."

Pursue the deeper mysteries of the Spirit

PATHS OF EVER-INCREASING GLORY

What Enoch's Ancient Writings Reveal about Christ's Supremacy and our Prophetic Destiny

MICHAEL FICKESS

PURCHASE YOUR COPY AT
WWW.MORNINGSTARMINISTRIES.ORG

Now in One Volume!

What if a single revelation could change your destiny in a moment? In this riveting bestselling series, author Rick Joyner takes you on the supernatural journey that has captivated millions. More real than an allegory, The Final Quest Trilogy is a panoramic vision of the epic struggle between light and darkness, and your part in it.

**PURCHASE YOUR COPY AT
WWW.MORNINGSTARMINISTRIES.ORG**

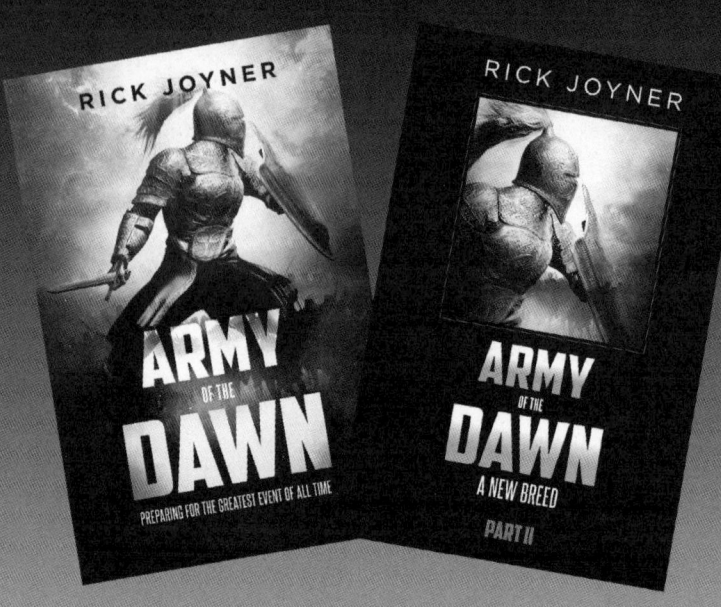

Army of the Dawn

by
Rick Joyner

Order Now
www.MorningStarMinistries.org/store
(800) 529-1117

TAKE CHARGE OF YOUR
DESTINY
CHANGE THE WORLD

MSU
MORNINGSTAR UNIVERSITY

Get More Information Today:
Visit MStarU.com

MorningStar
PARTNERS
— WORKING TOGETHER IN THE HARVEST —

A powerful spiritual army is now mobilizing. The earth is poised to receive the greatest impact from the Gospel ever seen. We need Partners who will join with us to raise up some of the most high-impact ministries in church history.

Join us in equipping the body of Christ here and around the world through our missions, conferences, schools, television, and books. You can become a MorningStar Partner with a regular contribution of any amount, whether it's once a month or once a year.

MorningStar Partners:
- Get the inside scoop with a free monthly subscription to *The MorningStar Journal*
- Connect with other Partners at exclusive events
- Participate in live webinars
- Save money with numerous discounts
- And more...

Partner With Us Today:

MStarPartners.org
Or Call 1.803.547.8495